ALSO BY JAMES BRUNO

TRIBE
PERMANENT INTERESTS
CHASM
HAVANA QUEEN

THE FOREIGN CIRCUS

Why Foreign Policy Should Not Be Left in
the Hands of Diplomats, Spies and
Political Hacks

BY

JAMES BRUNO

THE FOREIGN CIRCUS, by James Bruno

First Edition, April 2014

Copyright © 2013 James Bruno

This work has been reviewed and cleared by the U.S. Department of State. The opinions and characterizations in this book are those of the author and do not necessarily reflect official positions of the United States Government.

The following are personal views of the author. Any resemblance to persons living or dead is strictly coincidental.

Author services provided by Pedernales Publishing, LLC.
www.pedernalespublishing.com

For information email angkor456000@yahoo.com or contact:

Bittersweet House Press
P.O. Box 306
Canastota, NY 13035

ISBN: 978-0-9837642-8-1 Paperback Edition

ISBN: 978-0-9837642-9-8 Digital Edition

Printed in the United States of America

To the two hundred forty-four American diplomats who have sacrificed their lives in the line of duty

How is the world ruled and how do wars start? Diplomats tell lies to journalists and then believe what they read.

Karl Kraus

FOREWORD

Upon returning to Washington following my first three years as a junior Foreign Service officer and two overseas tours of duty, I reported to my "Career Development Officer," the State Department's fancy name for a personnel or human resources officer. As I sat at the foot of his desk, the CDO pored over my personnel file. He scrunched his brow as he turned the pages. Then he slowly shook his head. Finally, he looked up at me. "Well, Jim, let's face it. At your next posting, you'll need to hit the ground running." I asked him what he meant exactly. My supervisors had given me glowing appraisals and I'd been promoted quickly. "Let's be frank, Jim," he said. "Your performance hasn't been very good." I interrupted him and demanded to view the file myself. CDO Man initially hesitated, but forked it over as I stood and loomed over him. I examined the file. While the file cover had my name on it, the contents belonged to another officer. Somebody had misfiled. Incensed, I told CDO Man to get his act together and call me once he'd found my file. At this point, I knew something was wrong with this outfit. Twenty more years lay ahead of me.

The Chargé d'Affaires and political section chief at one embassy in which I'd served obliviously partied and dined with one of the Drug Enforcement Administration's top ten most wanted narcotraffickers. An ambassador I'd worked for ordered embassy staff to travel into the lawless interior of the civil war-torn country where guerrillas were targeting and assassinating foreigners, an order the staff refused. I witnessed how money bundlers and political hacks scarfed up posh diplomatic postings based on such things as size and lavishness of the ambassadorial residences. When I joined fellow Foreign Service and CIA colleagues in questioning a policy which had the Pakistanis diverting the bulk of U.S.-supplied armaments to radical Afghan Islamist guerrillas during the war against Soviet occupation, our superiors told us to sit down, shut up and do our jobs. I saw Caspar Milquetoast family men lose it in sexual playgrounds like Bangkok and Manila, ruining their marriages and relationships with their children. Ambassadors were not immune from this behavior. I watched as White House officials leaked classified information, then blamed the leaks on rank-and-file civil servants.

I've been pursued, surveilled, harassed, drugged, shot at, seized, jailed and denounced by the agents of hostile governments as well as a guerrilla movement. I required Uncle Sam's permission to marry. Our children were born in Africa and weaned in Asia. I served in a Secret Service presidential protection detail. All in all, it was an interesting career. So much so, that I left it early to write about it as a full-time author. My novels have been Amazon bestsellers and I've received national media attention ranging from

NBC's Today Show to *The Washington Post*. It's been a wild ride. So I've written about it here, my first nonfiction work, drawn from my blog, "Diplo Denizen." I sincerely hope you enjoy my stories half as much as I've had in putting them to paper. *The Foreign Circus*, a play on the words the Foreign Service, is a largely, though not exclusively, set of satirical commentaries on foreign policy, diplomacy and espionage and those who work in those spheres. I end with some insights on these subjects as well as on being a writer.

A Special Note on Censored Text

As a former official of the federal government with top secret clearances, I am required to submit for security review to the U.S. Department of State all of my writings prior to publication in order to protect what government reviewers deem sensitive information. It is my aim to present readers with as authentic insights as I can into the workings of our national security apparatus without violating mandated safeguards on classified information. I do not, however, submit to gratuitous censorship. The clearance process is one of negotiation between author and official reviewers in which I have the readers' interests and enjoyment at heart. You will see sentences and whole passages of blacked-out text (or X-ed out, in the case of older e-readers) in *The Foreign Circus*. This text was redacted by official censors who judged it too sensitive for public dissemination.

Contents

THE
FOREIGN
CIRCUS

THE U.S. FOREIGN SERVICE: PROMOTIONS, DERANGEMENT & SPOILS

How to Get Ahead in the U.S. Foreign Service: Walk, Don't Run

Ambition is the last refuge of failure. ~ Oscar Wilde

We Still Need Kremlinologists

After twenty-three years working for the Department of State, I left with little more understanding on how to get ahead in that opaque and byzantine system than I had upon entering. Yet, using my past kremlinologist skills as well as drawing from a long career of trying to decipher other closed regimes such as North Korea, Cuba and Chicago, I've come away with some pointers for those just entering the Department as well as those still inside the belly of the beast. Following are some broad type categorizations for success in the U.S. Foreign Service:

The Operator: Ratko Mladic, the Serbian war criminal now in being tried in The Hague, was an Operator. He embraced three keys for being a highly successful executive: (a) effective networking; (b) sucking up to his superiors; and (c) amorality and ruthlessness. So is it in the Foreign

Service. The effective Operator spreads his tentacles out the minute he completes his oath to protect and defend the Constitution. Think of the kiss-ass schmoozer we all knew in school. The brown-nose apple polisher who was at his teachers' feet and his classmates' throats. Like Mladic, such people are able to advance quickly, even if it's over a mountain of their victims' skulls. Definition of success per the Operator: *To crush your enemies, see them driven before you, and to hear the lamentations of their women and children!*

The Female Emasculator: Why is it that four decades on in the feminist movement, many women feel they must out-testosterone their male competition? Everyone is familiar with this ilk: the "barracuda" who devours her young if it will lead to advancement. The alpha-female who, if she sacrifices any time at all to romance, weds an emasculated Caspar Milquetoast – another pelt on the barn door. Most, however, don't marry. After all, matrimony and children only get in the way on the ladder-climb to victory. These women are the first to launch class action lawsuits claiming "discrimination" as a vehicle to win court-ordered promotions or plum assignments. Give them a wide berth; otherwise, find a fine surgeon to extricate the daggers and high-heel marks from your back and to reaffix your testicles.

Boobs Struck by Lightning: Think of the dumb-ass who can't organize his breakfast, constantly loses his keys, comes to work with one brown shoe and one black. Yet karmic lightning strikes and next thing you know he's in the fast lane, screwing up one assignment after another, yet continually rewarded as others pick up the pieces. A variation on this species is the "Being There" type, patterned after the eponymous Peter Sellers movie. The protagonist, named Chance, is a simpleton who, because he dresses like an aristocrat and says little, is fawned over and rewarded by pompous social climbers who are blind to his vacuousness. Form trumps substance.

The Anointed One: Similar to Boobs Struck by Lightning minus the dumbassedness. This is the individual who is visited by Jesus while in A-100 junior officer training and thereafter put on the super-fast track despite never having an original idea, being devoid of personality and showing all the risk-taking of a Swiss accountant. The Old Boys just like him/her and coddle the haloed Anointed One through unremarkable ambassadorships and snoozer sinecures up to the Undersecretary level.

The Wagon-Hitcher: A bevy of these often capable FSO's rode on the coattails of Henry Kissinger to the pinnacles of the foreign policy establishment. Finding oneself attached to such a shooting star is as often as not a factor of dumb luck, being at the right place at the right time with the right senior official on the way to megastar status. These Wagon-Hitchers become luminaries in their own right and enjoy highly successful careers. *There but for the grace of God go I…*

Get Along to Go Along: Those with severe CDD (Charisma Deficit Disorder), a face in the crowd and a harmless, nonthreatening disposition who do their time in the bowels of the bureaucracy accomplishing little more but staying in place and offending no one often are rewarded in their

50s with an ambassadorship to a malarial backwater capital shunned by the parvenu political appointees (see *The American Diplomatic Spoils System: Embassies for Sale*). It's the State Department's version of the gold watch.

Lateral (No Exam Required) Entry: This means of advancement, which exempts its beneficiaries from such inconveniences as the Foreign Service exam, is reserved for cronies and affirmative action entrants.

Legacy: Just as the Ivy League traditionally reserves admission spaces for the offspring of distinguished alumni (remember Pres. W?), the Foreign Service takes special care to coddle and promote the careers of the children of distinguished Foreign Service officers. If you are a Foreign Service brat, your odds at finding yourself on the fast track are greater than the peons, particularly if dad was an ambassador.

Caution and Incompetence

In my first Department posting, as I rushed down one of the long gray corridors with a draft cable in hand to seek an urgent clearance at another office, a stooped, pasty-faced FSO admonished me, "Walk, don't run!" I think the last person to scold me thus was Miss Nall, my sixth grade teacher. But over the years I found it to be emblematic of the careful, cautious, compromising Foreign Service culture; of waiting one's turn, not rocking the boat, staying in lock-step, all keys to that ambassadorial posting to Lower Slobovia.

After my first overseas tour, I went to pay an obligatory call on my "Career Development Officer." As I sat silently, this man thumbed through my file, brows scrunched, grave demeanor. As he read on, he began to shake his head. Then he looked up at me and said, "Let's face it, Jim. You're going to have to hit the ground running in your next assignment." I was stunned. I had gotten nothing but sterling evaluations. I said, "What do you mean?" The CDO shrugged and frowned. "Well, you didn't do so well in your first tour, did you?" I stood up and requested to have a look at my file. He reluctantly handed it to me. While the folder had my name on it, the contents belonged to another officer. My personnel papers had been misfiled. Steaming, I demanded that the CDO straighten it out and call me as soon as he did. It was an early lesson in the fallibilities of the personnel system.

Operators, Boobs, Emasculators and all the Rest

To be successful as an **Operator**, one must have an ego the size of time. Throw in a messiah complex, narcissism and a Teflon-coated conscience and the picture is complete. As a young consulate chief, my boss, the embassy's deputy chief of mission (DCM), spent every waking minute expounding on what a magnificent officer he was, how he performed flawless language interpretation for a U.S. president (funny, presidents always bring their own professional interpreters), and what an outstanding expert he was in this, that and the other thing. In his spare time, when not saving the globe from certain destruction, he wrote a how-to book with his wife. Yadda, yadda. Indeed, this self-centered blowhard was promoted as ambassador to an important country where he went around mouthing off about his many attributes in as many languages as he could muster. Finally, his wife had had enough and divorced him. His oversized self-esteem did him in on a scuttled appointment to a senior job after he severely attacked a U.S. ally and was found to have questionable, conflict-of-interest financial ties to countries he had worked in. Lesson for the would-be Operator: there is a line that can be crossed at one's peril, even for the insufferable, out-of-control egomaniac.

One of the most incompetent officials I'd ever known was a man whose secretaries quit because they couldn't keep up with his disorganization. A Kissinger acolyte recruited him to be his deputy chief of mission at a large embassy. There, he drove the embassy staff crazy by creating one organizational mess after another. Morale sank while this **Boob** mismanaged the place like a sugar-o.d'd kindergartner. What did the Department do with him after he practically destroyed an embassy? It named him to be a Special Envoy! His drooping posture and stammering delivery turned off the foreign officials he was supposed to lobby. His aide, a young FSO, complained bitterly that he constantly lost his classified briefing papers, air tickets, bags and even his underwear. This Special Envoy regularly flubbed up his message to foreign counterparts. Like the emperor with no clothes, this nebbish of a man's incompetencies were evident to all but himself and the fools who repeatedly promoted him.

The woman I succeeded in one of my Washington jobs was a foul-tempered, mean-spirited misanthrope with a permanent sneer plastered on her witch's face. She refused to help me read into my new job and left classified papers in the messy desk I inherited from her, leading to my being cited for a security violation after my first day on the job. ███████████████████████████████████████, I managed to torpedo it as well as her follow-on assignment after talking to some friends in the assignments office. I followed suit with the misanthrope woman as well, leading to her being sidelined for a couple of years. I've had superb female bosses and coworkers. The **Emasculator** is to be found in all organizations. Fortunately, they are the exception and not the rule.

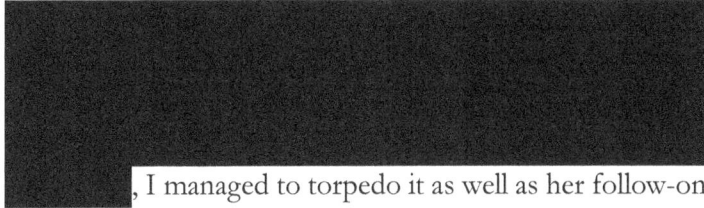

I once worked for an **Anointed One**, a golden boy whom good fortune repeatedly visited during his long and prestigious career. Son of an army general, he was bright, charming and very likeable. But he was not a taskmaster in his very senior position and felt put upon whenever asked to dirty his hands with earth-bound tasks such as personnel matters. And he remained aloof from the Washington social scene, thus forfeiting power networking which is a hallmark for political success. During my two pleasant years as this man's aide, colleagues would quietly ask me, "What makes him so successful?" While they recognized his competence, they saw little of the dynamic and forceful personality that usually characterizes executives of his stature. I wanted to answer, "He was visited by Jesus during junior officer training." But I waffled, ever the loyal servant. The Anointed Ones are very few, but they somehow float to the top.

Most FSO's who win the coveted title of Ambassador do so by playing it safe, laboring hard in the trenches of a geographic bureau, **Getting Along to Go Along**, posing a threat to no one, being good team players. These people patiently wait decades for their reward, a small or medium-sized embassy in Africa, Asia or other third world outpost that the political appointees find distasteful and therefore leave to the careerists. They get to carry the title of ambassador for life, which often gets them a post-retirement job teaching at a podunk college in the Midwest.

The Foreign Service exam is a battery of rigorous tests through which candidates must compete in order to become one of the few selected each year to be a U.S. Foreign Service officer. This gauntlet, however, is seen as a barrier to some whom the Department needs or wants to hire either for diversity reasons or to bring in a senior official's cronies. Race, ethnicity, gender, physical handicaps, handedness, height, eye color, surgical scars, sexual orientation, musical talent, Elvis impersonations, you-name-it can get you in the side door. Yet another pathway to entrance and advancement.

A notorious case of a **Lateral Entry** crony was "Psycho-DAS." An Assistant Secretary of State for a regional bureau had a pal who was trained as a psychologist, but made a living as owner of a B&B and writing really bad thriller novels on the side. This man, who lacked any international affairs or diplomatic training, was hired to be a Deputy Assistant Secretary (DAS) at his friend's insistence. The Department went along, shelling out big bucks to get him a security clearance. In charge of a geographic sub-region, "Psycho-DAS," as he came to be known, was lost at sea, having not a clue as to how to carry out a job career FSO's compete hard to get after many years in the trenches. Psycho-DAS sat in his office and wandered the halls, merely taking up space. Employees speculated that he got the job in order to gather material for his pedestrian novels. The whole sordid affair underscored one form of corruption that goes on in the Department, one that should have gotten media and congressional attention. Psycho-DAS left quietly after a brief and unproductive diplomatic stint.

I encountered **Legacy** favoritism in its most egregious and shameless form when I served in the so-called "Mother Bureau" of State, "EUR" – European Affairs. There, I got to participate in the so-called Meat Market, which is the colloquial term for the assignments committee. The Meat Market is State's version of politics' "smoke-filled room" of yore. Who goes where is sorted out in this free-form cabal. The decision of whom to put forth as the bureau's candidate to a Balkan DCM-ship came up. The name of a Department-based desk officer for a Balkan country was on the short list. Known among the rank-and-file as "Mr. F--k-up," for his disorganization, failure to meet deadlines and slovenly appearance, I explained in careful language the man's many weaknesses as well as some of his strengths. One of the Deputy Assistant Secretaries piped up, "{Name} is the son of Ambassador {Name}. We must take care of him." In fact, Mr. F--k-up's dad himself had been ambo to a Balkan nation. Indeed, son previously had followed in dad's footsteps as Legacy at an Ivy League university. Legacy trumped ability and Mr. F--k-up went on to a highly successful career riding on his old man's coattails and Old Boy connections.

Wizards & Star Chambers

The Foreign Service promotion process used to be totally opaque. Senior officers would write evaluations on FSO's and their wives (female FSO's were required to resign upon marrying under the old double standard system) with no opportunity for input from the latter. Assignments were made equally opaquely. One simply received assignment orders and went. Reforms were instituted. Employee evaluations are a two-way process. Employees may also lobby for their onward assignments in a program called the Open Assignments Process. Trouble is, it is neither open nor a process but Mafia-like backroom wheeling and dealing whereby senior officials ensure their loyal subalterns are justly rewarded with Paris or Berlin, while those without connections are left with Port Moresby and Ouagadougou. Ambassadorships, deputy chiefs of missions and heads of consulates are likewise selected in star chambers presided over by veteran diplo-wizards. After carefully adhering to diversity requisites, the wizards then distribute the spoils in accordance with age-old tribal loyalties, rice-bowl equities and favors owed. I was twice the beneficiary of this system, which I nonetheless detested. Further reform is necessary.

Alchemy, Luck & Dysfunction

Every large organization has dysfunctionalities. And getting to the top is at least two-parts alchemy and luck. There's no one sure way to success. Many factors come into play. The Foreign Service and Department of State are no exceptions. But in government, where there is no "bottom line" or other standard to empirically gauge employees' effectiveness, the dysfunctionality quotient has a greater influence on who is rewarded and who is not. State Department lore is rife with the likes of Psycho-DAS, rapacious Emasculators, cutthroat Operators and Boobs with a license to foul up. You can't make this stuff up. It's a major catalyst that drove me to write fiction. And it's one reason that my novels continue to be bestsellers – authenticity. I wish I were an Anointed One, but Jesus overlooked me in A-100 training.

Running Amok: Mental Health in the U.S. Foreign Service

Ship me somewhere's east of Suez, where the best is like the worst. Where there aren't no ten commandments, an' a man can raise a thirst. ~ Rudyard Kipling, Mandalay

Amok

In the second year of my Foreign Service career, I was assigned to Vientiane, Laos. My deployment was accelerated by my predecessor's seeking and being granted a one-year curtailment of his tour of duty because he was going bonkers. Moreover, an admin officer had to be removed in a straitjacket after holing himself up in his house and smearing the walls with his own feces, another victim of mental and emotional stress. I, on the other hand, thrived at this isolated outpost, our only one in Indochina five years

following the fall of Saigon. The setting was a cross between "Heart of Darkness" and "Casablanca." My seizure
at gunpoint and brief incarceration by the authorities, which
prompted a diplomatic row, was just one of the pressures
at this surreal place. Years later, in civil war-torn Cambodia,
the State Department regularly sent a psychiatrist to post to
measure our stress levels amid coup attempts, assassinations,
12-14-hour work days seven days a week and an unhinged
ambassador. At another embassy, one of our largest, the
Secretary of State discreetly sent out two senior officials to
gently pry our prominent career ambassador out of his job
in the wake of his increasingly bizarre behavior, including
public denunciations of an American ally.

PTSD on the Rise

There is a popular perception of diplomats as wan angora-
stroking effetes whose greatest challenge of the day is
cocktails at the tennis club. This couldn't be farther from
the truth. The stress of serving in isolated poverty-ridden
countries and war zones can be tremendous. Family members are not allowed at many of these posts, resulting in
so-called unaccompanied tours. Children are sometimes required to be separated from parents and placed in overseas
boarding schools.

In recent years, the number of Foreign Service personnel
medevacced for mental health reasons has doubled. One
study revealed 15 percent of FS members suffered from
PTSD. A similar study done by the Defense Department
found that 17 percent of soldiers returned from Iraq and

Afghanistan suffered from the same condition. As the U.S. has gotten involved in more overseas conflicts, the pressures on our diplomats have compounded.

A particularly sad case was documented in the September 2010 issue of the Foreign Service Journal. A former military officer and tsunami survivor, this FSO was assigned to one of the most dangerous war zones six years into his State Department career. He worked 12-14-hour days amid gun and mortar fire. After being injured in a roadside bomb attack, a State Department psychiatrist prescribed an antidepressant for his PTSD. But the medication caused lack of sleep, loss of appetite and high blood pressure. When he complained about the side effects, he was prescribed a different antidepressant. But the side effects continued and he was evacuated from post and placed in psychiatric hospitalization in Washington. State Department's MED office failed to provide him with a doctor proficient in treating PTSD, so he found one on his own. He was told he could not return to post. Further treatment did not resolve his problem and he was medevacced again from another post. He lives in Washington, separated from his wife, and essentially grounded for medical reasons. His career prospects don't look good. This officer is convinced that, had he received better treatment, his current situation could have been avoided.

Mental Health Treatment Can Be Bad for Your Career

The growing concern in the Foreign Service ranks over mental health problems prompted former Secretary Clinton to assure employees that they can and should seek treatment by State Department medical professionals with no worry that it would impact negatively on their careers. But a loose grouping of FS professionals calling themselves Concerned Foreign Service Officers has strongly urged U.S. diplomats to seek needed psychiatric help from private practitioners rather than from State Department doctors. "CFSO has seen numerous cases where even allegations of mental health issues, ranging from PTSD to depression to marital discord to stress-related substance abuse have been referred by M/MED to Diplomatic Security (DS), usually resulting in recommendations to revoke a clearance." In other words, if you seek treatment for a mental health issue, you risk losing your security clearances, which is definitely a career-killer. The upshot? Those with PTSD, substance abuse issues, depression, etc. refusing to seek treatment for fear it would stifle their career.

The Best is Like the Worst

A Foreign Service career is not for the faint of heart. The threat of terrorism, disease, isolation and sheer mental exhaustion is prevalent. And as we shift more human resources to places like Afghanistan and Iraq, as well as Africa, the Middle East and other troubled areas, the greater the stress on American envoys. Cocktails at the tennis club? Sorry, I've got a war to cover.

The American Diplomatic Spoils System, Part I: Embassies for Sale

A Foreign Service career takes the guts out of people.
~ Ambassador Evan Galbraith, political appointee

The Spoils System

An often told story in the State Department has it that former ambassador to Turkey and Pakistan Ron Spiers was a guest on a U.S. aircraft carrier in the Persian Gulf some years ago. The admiral who hosted him remarked that after he retired, he was thinking of getting himself appointed as an ambassador. Spiers reportedly rejoined that after retiring he was thinking of getting himself named as an admiral in charge of the Sixth Fleet. "But it takes decades of training and highly specialized knowledge to command a fleet," the astonished Navy man replied. "So does running an embassy," Spiers reportedly shot back.

The United States is the only industrialized country to sell its ambassadorships to the highest bidders in an outmoded diplomatic spoils system that rivals any such corruption in any banana republic, dictatorship or two-bit monarchy. Military flag officer positions were similarly sold up until the end of the civil war when the public recoiled at the extent of needless slaughter brought on by incompetent politically appointed generals like Daniel Sickles, whose insubordination at the Battle of Gettysburg caused over 4,000 Union casualties. Congress outlawed the practice of military patronage. But ambassadorships continue to be available to any moneyed dolt with party connections.

In the last sixty years, 72 percent of U.S. ambassadorial posts in Western Europe and the Caribbean have gone to political appointees while 86 percent of such positions in Africa and the Middle East have gone to career diplomats, according to the American Foreign Service Association (AFSA). Of twelve choice ambassadorships in Europe and the Caribbean, the average amount raised for each is now $1.79 million.

Rogue's Gallery

In an earlier commentary ("Love, Romance & Sex in the U.S. Foreign Service - Part I: Of Lust & Loneliness"), I suggested that someone needs to collect 200 years of lore on the idiots who are allowed to buy United States ambassadorships. I haven't done that, but here is just a sampling of some of the most memorable idiots and their disservice to their country:

Joseph Kennedy, a major donor to Democrats in the 1930s and President Franklin Roosevelt's ambassador to Britain, resigned in disgrace after proclaiming democracy "finished in England" in the wake of Adolf Hitler's early victories in WWII. Another Roosevelt appointee, wealthy financier Bernard Baruch's brother, caused sex scandals while serving as ambassador to Portugal and again when he was transferred to the Netherlands.

In fact, ambassadorial sexcapades feature prominently among this crowd:

Former U.S. Ambassador to Norway Mark Evans Austad, an outspoken former Mormon missionary who hurled verbal attacks against a variety of Norwegian liberal institutions as well as the press was taken by police at a house where he was bellowing loudly and banging on a woman's door at 3 a.m. Austad claimed that, after hosting a cocktail party, he headed to a friend's house "to plan a salmon fishing trip," and the taxi had taken him to the wrong address. The police returned Austad to his residence.

Joseph Zappala, a wealthy Florida developer and fundraiser for President George H.W. Bush, was appointed ambassador to Spain despite his inability to speak Spanish. Zappala's tour in Madrid was marred when he took up with another woman, ending his thirty-year marriage. "This guy's roaming eye for the Spanish ladies became very embarrassing for us in the career Foreign Service," said someone who served in Madrid under Zappala.

Otherwise, many incompetent politically appointed ambassadors distinguish themselves by mere public embarrassments and varying levels of damage to U.S. foreign policy:

In the late 1980s, our ambassador to Italy was an Italian-American lumber baron from Minnesota, Pete Secchia. Having donated generously to his party, Secchia got the job, though he possessed no diplomatic or related experience. An otherwise gregarious sort, he was at sea in Rome. He used one of the most sensitive communications channels, normally reserved for matters of high policy, to update the Secretary of State on his project to remodel Villa Taverna, the U.S. ambassador's residence, including one lengthy cable on his selection of curtains. He was also fond of telling demeaning Italian jokes before crowds of host country officials and journalists, an act that endeared neither him nor the United States to the Italian public.

Jimmy Carter's ambassador to Singapore, a former South Dakota state legislator, walked off with the ambassadorial china upon completion of his unremarkable assignment. Upon being asked to return the expensive, eagle-embossed dinnerware, our ambassador refused, stating it was his just reward for having been an ambassador.

And then there's the peculiar case of William A. Wilson, Ronald Reagan's friend and the first U.S. ambassador to the Vatican. In January of 1986, Wilson embarked on an unauthorized diplomatic mission to Libya and secretly met with Libyan strongman Muammar Gaddafi in an effort to open relations between the two countries. Secretary of State George Shultz officially reprimanded Wilson.

Evan Galbraith, a wealthy non-French-speaking investment banker who served as Reagan's first ambassador to France, may have set a record by receiving four formal protests from the French foreign ministry, the last for an interview he gave in 1985 in which he slammed the government of President Francois Mitterrand for inviting Communist ministers in his Cabinet and in which he enthusiastically predicted that the ruling Socialist Party would go down in defeat in the upcoming French elections. Not exactly a team player, Galbraith, too, was publicly rebuked by Shultz for stating that a Foreign Service career "takes the guts out of people."

Another potential trap for inexperienced diplomats is "clientitis," or identifying too closely with the host country while losing sight of U.S. policy interests. An egregious example of "going native" was U.S. Ambassador to Romania James Rosapepe, a Clinton appointee who came under fire in a report by the State Department's inspector general. The report charged Rosapepe with failing to inform Washington of developments in Romania, becoming too identified with Romanian policies, exercising poor judgment by including Romanian nationals in embassy meetings, and by excluding U.S. diplomats from high-level meetings with Romanian leaders. Rosapepe's information was so biased that "we really have no idea what is going on there," the inspector general's report stated.

Likewise, many prominent socialites are frequently named to plush postings such as Barbados, which welcomed real estate heiress Joy Silverman — a Bush Sr. appointee who lacked a college degree — and U.S. Ambassador Mary Ourisman — a Bush Jr. appointee and Texas-born socialite and wife of a prominent Washington automobile dealer.

Perhaps the most embarrassing and needlessly self-inflicted ambassadorial political appointment was that of California hotel magnate Larry Lawrence as President Clinton's envoy to Switzerland. At the time of his nomination, Lawrence had more than two dozen cases pending against him in federal tax court, prompting the American Foreign Service Association to issue an unusual and unsuccessful demand that he not be confirmed. Lawrence died in 1996 and received a waiver to be buried at Arlington National Cemetery based on his claim of having been wounded during WWII while serving in the Merchant Marines. Later, it was discovered that he never served in the Merchant Marines and that much of the rest of his life story was also fabricated. Ultimately, his body was exhumed and reburied in San Diego, and the Justice Department launched an investigation into how the State Department and White House failed to catch Lawrence's many lies during his background check.

Obama's Dilettantes

As with many newly elected presidents of an idealistic bent, Barack Obama stated that he would place more emphasis on appointing career diplomats to ambassadorial posts. In the first six months of his first term, Obama sent to the Senate 58 ambassadorial nominations. Of those 32, or 55 percent, were political appointees. In the same time period, his five predecessors made more nominations — an average of 67 — but the number of those who were political was lower at 47 percent. In President Obama's second term, 37 percent of all ambassadorial positions have gone to noncareer appointees, close to a record. Oh, well.

Following is just a partial roster of the neophytes Obama has sent to top diplomatic postings in return for large payoffs in the form of "bundled" campaign contributions that circumvent the spirit, if not the letter, of campaign finance laws:

- John Roos for Japan. Roos is a California lawyer and campaign fundraiser, raising at least $500,000 for Obama's campaign; moreover, he and his immediate family gave $41,600 in campaign contributions, including $4,600 to Obama.
- Louis Susman, for the United Kingdom in 2008. A former Citigroup VP who raised $300,000 for Obama and contributed $50,000 for Obama's inauguration.
- Charles Rivkin was given the Paris ambassadorial post. A former financial analyst at Salomon Brothers, he raised $800,000 for Obama in 2008.
- Insurance lawyer Allan Katz was given the Lisbon ambassadorial post in return for having raised $500,000 in Obama's 2008 campaign.
- Laurie Fulton was made ambassador to Denmark. A corporate lawyer who runs a California entertainment company, she raised up to $200,000 for Obama and contributed $4,100 to Obama's 2008 campaign.
- Mathew Barzun, Obama's campaign finance chairman, was made ambassador to London after he raised $2.3 million for Obama's 2012 re-election campaign.
- Rome went to John Phillips, a Washington lawyer who raised $500,000 for Obama's 2012 campaign.
- John Emerson was made ambassador to Germany after he raised $1.5 million in 2012.

Marie Antoinette of the Ardennes: The Terrible Cynthia Stroum

Poor little Grand Duchy of Luxembourg. Considered a throw-away country by the White House, this Rhode Island-sized NATO ally has always been the dumping ground for the flightiest of politically appointed U.S. ambassadors. Real estate magnates without a cause. Airhead socialites without a clue about foreign policy. Connected car salesmen who want to play Statesman for a couple of years. The Luxembourgeois have seen them come and go. Unlike our political leadership, these proud folks do not view themselves as marionettes in a toy fairytale land. They participated in the D-Day invasion and were a founding member of both the UN and the EU. They grudgingly tolerate the idiots we send as our envoys while getting the real business done through our professional diplomats and directly in Washington.

In 2009, President Obama sent as his ambassador Cynthia Stroum, a wealthy Seattle investor who raised $500,000 for Obama, putting her near the top of the campaign's rainmakers. That's $1 for every Luxembourg citizen.

She abruptly resigned one year later, just after the State Department's inspector general issued a blistering report stating the embassy "has underperformed for the entirety of the current ambassador's tenure." The report went on to describe the ambassador's managerial style as fraught with personality conflicts, verbal abuse and questionable expenditures on travel and booze. "At present, due to internal problems, it plays no significant role in policy advocacy or reporting, though developments in Luxembourg are certainly of interest to Washington clients and other U.S. missions in the NATO and EU communities."

Ambassador Stroum had so terrorized her small staff that the inspector general recommended the State Department dispatch medical personnel to examine the stress levels of embassy employees. It noted at least four quit or sought transfers to Iraq and Afghanistan during her tenure, rare actions for diplomats at a cushy European post.

"The bulk of the mission's internal problems are linked to her leadership deficiencies, the most damaging of which is an abusive management style," the report said. "She has followed a pattern of public criticism of colleagues, including (deputies), who have not performed to her satisfaction …Those who have questioned or challenged some of the ambassador's actions state that they have paid a heavy price in the form of verbal abuse and been threatened with dismissal," it said.

Shortly after her arrival, Stroum stressed "the importance she attaches to the perquisites of" being an ambassador. She was particularly concerned about the state of the ambassador's residence, then under renovation, it said. To locate temporary housing for her, an embassy officer spent six weeks searching for a suitable abode, investigating 200 properties. Only four met the ambassador's requirements and she rejected them all, according to the report, before an acceptable residence finally was found.

In violation of the regs, Stroum spent $2,400 of embassy funds to fly with an aide to a Swiss "professional school" which has sent graduates to work at Buckingham Palace to interview candidates to replace a retired property caretaker and a fired chef. The trip was disguised as "management meetings."

The embassy purchased $3,400 in wine and liquor a day before the 2010 budget year ended, another violation of the rules. The embassy paid for the purchase of a new ambassadorial bed because Stroum "preferred a queen bed to the king-size bed already provided."

Fleshpots and Backwaters

Transgressions by noncareer ambassadors include cocaine smuggling using diplomatic pouches, drunken imbroglios at embassy functions, embarrassing adulterous affairs, and simple ineptitude. The above cases represent a mere random sampling and fraction of the incompetence and embarrassment brought on by the diplomatic spoils system.

The upshot is that the attractive and important posts of Europe, Asia and the Caribbean are sold to moneybag charlatans, leaving malarial war zones and forgotten backwaters to the career people. What's most pathetic is the lengths to which career FSOs fight over these scraps. Men and women who would make outstanding envoys to Berlin, Tokyo and Ottawa battle like junkyard dogs to be named ambassador to Lower Slobovia.

This is not to say that all career Foreign Service officers make good managers. In fact, most are not. The Department lore is rife with tales, past and present, of so-called "super political officers" who can name every member of Kyrgyzstan's government cabinet but who couldn't, as recounted about former Iraq czar Paul Bremer, "organize a two-car funeral." I could list here many more cases of career officers who were as damaging, incompetent, crazy and clueless as any political appointee. I'm thinking of devoting a separate commentary to that subject (see "Why I Write" for a couple of examples). But a person with years of relevant training and experience certainly wins hands-down over the dilettante.

Administrations use a variety of excuses to masquerade the practice of selling ambassadorships, the most common one being that an envoy who enjoys direct access to the President can be the most effective. This is utter hogwash. Ambassadors' chain of command goes through the Secretary of State. Going outside of that chain is cause for confusion and misunderstandings and is actually frowned upon by White House and State Department officials alike.

Guts

As for a Foreign Service career "taking the guts out of people," apparently Ambassador Galbraith was unaware of the (now) 244 U.S. diplomats who have given their lives in the line of duty, including Terrence L. Barnich who was killed by a roadside bomb in Iraq on Memorial Day 2009. All 244 names are prominently displayed on memorial plaques in the Department's main entrance; hard to miss as one enters the building.

But…yes. You too can become a United States ambassador! The American Dream can be yours – with a bag of swag and the proper arse-kissing.

The American Diplomatic Spoils System, Part II: Election's Over - Let the Spoils Begin!

Dear Mr. President:

First, congratulations on your re-election. Great job! Second, you may recall that I had written about our country's diplomatic spoils system last year. Since you no doubt already are being inundated with bids for ambassadorships from a bevy of party hacks, money bundlers, airhead society dames and vulture capitalists, I thought I'd waste no time putting in my recommendations. So, here they are:

Scrooge McDuck

A charter member of the Billionaire's Club of Duckburg, Mr. McDuck is emblematic of the American Dream: a rags-to-riches immigrant who represents an underserved minority: Scottish-Americans. McDuck, who made his fortune in socially responsible and green sectors, including selling fridges to Inuit and wind to windmill manufacturers, out gave his Republican rival, John D. Rockerduck, to the Democrat super PAC, Fowl Play America. His nephews, Huey, Dewey and Louie, moreover, have been active in energizing the youth *wing* of Duckburg's Democratic *flock*. He is a member of the board of Disney. The multilingual McDuck is requesting to be named America's first ambassador to breakaway Scotland.

Curly Howard

Affectionately called "Knucklehead" by his associates, Moe and Larry, Curly Howard led the Tinsel Town effort to re-elect you, Mr. President. An Academy Award nominee for his films, *Halfwit Holiday*, *We Want Our Mummy* and *Disorder in the Court*, Curly went mansion-to-mansion in Beverly Hills batter-ramming each door with his head until the homeowner responded, whereupon Curly ran in place, barked and did an elaborate knuckle-cracking routine until his targets coughed up cash for the Stooges for America super PAC. Curly knows how to say, nyuk-nyuk-nyuk in Ebonics, Yiddish and Pig Latin, thereby, qualifying him for the diplomatic life. His starring role in the Middle Eastern-themed *Malice in the Palace* and *Rumpus in the Harem* would make Curly ideally suited to be Middle East Envoy.

Gloria Teasdale & Rufus T. Firefly

An A-lister in the *Social Register*, Gloria Teasdale is well known to you, Mr. President, as a fixture at every significant soiree given in Washington since the Truman administration. Mrs. Teasdale is fortunate to already have had diplomatic experience along with her associate, Rufus T. Firefly. Mrs. Teasdale, you may recall, arranged for Firefly to be appointed leader of the small, bankrupt country of Freedonia as a condition for her continued provision of much-needed financial backing. This, unfortunately, led to a brief war with neighboring Sylvania, but all turned out well in the end under the unsteady, but determined stewardship of Mr. Firefly, who, speaking before the Cosmo Club, said, "I don't want to belong to any club that would have me as a member." Their daring saga was made into the dramatic film, *Duck Soup*. Mrs. Teasdale is requesting London, while the gregarious Mr. Firefly would be pleased to be named ambassador to the Court of St. James – now hang on…that is to say…uh…

Thurston Howell III

A member of the New England Yankee elite—a resident of Newport, Rhode Island and a graduate of Harvard University, Thurston Howell III was included in Forbes Magazine's 2006 list of the fifteen richest fictional characters. An avowed Republican, the venture capitalist nonetheless hedges his bets and gave generously to the Blue Dog Republicans for Obama super PAC. His wife, Lovey, gives charity benefits (Retired Polo Horse Foundation, Vintage Rolls Royce Museum and the America Cup Food Drive) and has a refined sense of noblesse oblige. Mr. Howell fills the bill of progressive plutocrat, and would be pleased to be given the Barbados ambassadorship so that he can go yachting twelve months of the year. His appointment would demonstrate the administration's commitment to bipartisanship.

So, this is my roster of diplomatic dilettantes thus far, Mr. President. I would unabashedly throw my own hat in the ring, but, alas, with three university degrees in international relations, twenty-three years as a Foreign Service officer and a modest bank account, I'm afraid that I am overqualified and underfunded. So, let's keep with the tried and true American political tradition of giving our country's most sought-after and prestigious ambassadorships to the vacuously wealthy, the intellectually challenged, and kiss-ass party agitprops. We eagerly await your first list of names to be submitted to the Senate for approval. And once appointed, we can all sleep soundly knowing our nation's foreign policy is in capable hands.

The American Diplomatic Spoils System, Part III: My Job Application to the World's Most Popular Soap Opera

To: Bradley Bell
        Executive Producer, CBS
        The Bold and the Beautiful

Dear Mr. Bell:

I hereby submit my application to join the cast of your wildly successful soap opera, The Bold and the Beautiful. After reading about your wife, Colleen, a producer for B&B, being named by President Obama to be our next ambassador to Hungary, I thought, I too, can realize one of my wildest dreams: become a soap opera matinée idol.

Now, looking at my résumé, you might think, "Hmm. Very thin. No acting experience. No background in showbiz. He's very good looking though!"

I know, I know. Yes, very thin indeed, with only twenty-five years working in the U.S. government foreign affairs establishment, twenty-three of those as a Foreign Service officer; seven years of higher education devoted to international relations, including at the U.S. Naval War College and an Ivy League university, I really have little to offer as a soap opera actor. And I'll confess I haven't watched a soap opera since my mother caught highlights of As the World Turns during breaks from housework when I was a little kid. But, having failed at getting my own presidential appointment to embassy Rome or Paris because political hack fundraisers always ace out career diplomats for these posts, I need to make a career change. I'm a bestselling thriller writer. That's not too far from showbiz, is it?

I figure if Colleen can become an ambassador with zero foreign affairs credentials, why shouldn't I be able to break into showbiz? After all, this is America, right? With all due respect to Mrs. Bell, who appears to be highly successful in Hollywood production and as a philanthropist and, of course, a political fundraiser, her diplomatic credentials are not only thin. They're nonexistent. Don't get me wrong. Being a trustee of the John F. Kennedy Center for the Performing Arts and having co-chaired an event celebrating World Oceans Day is nothing to sneeze at. And having hosted two events at your home for the Foo Fighters is indeed impressive ("Foo" what?). But I guess the real clincher centers on what has one done for the Pres. lately. The New York Times reports that Colleen Bell is one of Obama's top fundraisers, having raised $2,191,835 in 2011 and 2012.

'Fraid I can't compete with big bucks. But here's what I can offer to CBS's B&B. Hollywood and Foggy Bottom have much in common: plenty of contrived dramas, glitzy superficiality, fragile runaway egos, Machiavellian intrigues and backstabbing. I was immersed in this bizarre culture for two-and-a-half decades. It's all second nature to me. And here's how I propose you use it on your show once you've hired me on: write me in as J. Huntington Outerbridge III, an effete, conniving, snarky diplomat who sleeps with all the beautiful female characters while engaged in high-stakes diplomacy to foil nefarious plots by al-Qaida and the Iranian Revolutionary Guard. It's a winner! Watch your ratings go through the roof.

I eagerly await your call to audition.

P.S. --

TO: James Costos, HBO V-P chosen to be the next U.S. ambassador to Spain, and Charles Rivkin, ex-CEO of The Jim Henson Company, and recently U.S. ambassador to France:

My résumés are on the way!

On the First Line of Defense:
The Foreign Service

One of the first things they tell you in training to be a U.S. Foreign Service officer is that our embassies and consulates are the first line of defense for the country. This was proven tragically in Libya where Ambassador Chris Stevens and three U.S. diplomatic personnel were killed by extremists. They were indeed manning the front lines in the service of their country.

I worked for the last U.S. ambassador to have died in the line of duty, Arnold L. Raphel, who was killed in a plane crash, along with the President of Pakistan, in 1988. I still have an emotional reaction when I recall his moving burial ceremony at Arlington cemetery. He was forty-five years old.

At my last posting, Hanoi, Vietnam, nine military colleagues were killed in a helicopter crash. I stood at attention then too as their coffins were loaded onto aircraft for repatriation to the U.S. and their loved ones. Most Foreign Service employees probably knew, or know of, colleagues who had either died or were injured in the line of duty.

In the main lobby of the State Department are several marble plaques engraved with the names of 244 men and women who gave their lives representing the United States as diplomats. Eight of them were ambassadors. Now with the fatalities in Libya, we count 96 diplomats killed in the line of duty since 1981. The U.S. Foreign Service has some

12,000 employees. Like most of my colleagues, whenever I passed by those plaques on my way to the office, I reminded myself that my name could easily have joined the death roster while serving in dangerous places. There but for the grace of God…

I've written previously about a popular misperception among Americans about the nature of the work of U.S. diplomats. In "Running Amok: Mental Health in the U.S. Foreign Service," I noted that "the number of Foreign Service personnel medevacced for mental health reasons has doubled. One study revealed 15 percent of FS members suffered from PTSD. A similar study done by the Defense Department found that 17 percent of soldiers returned from Iraq and Afghanistan suffered from the same condition. As the U.S. has gotten involved in more overseas conflicts, the pressures on our diplomats have compounded."

Fueling the popular misperception of diplomats as effete cookie pushers are ignorant and malicious statements by some of our political leaders aimed at the Foreign Service. The non-career politically appointed ex-ambassador to France, Evan Galbraith, stated, "the Foreign Service takes the guts out of people." More recently, former presidential primary candidate, Rick Perry, spat, "I'm not sure our State Department serves us well" and went on to excoriate career Foreign Service officers.

Not long after Mr. Perry made his irresponsible attack against his country's diplomats, twenty-five-year old Anne Smedinghoff was killed by a suicide bomber in Afghanistan.

In the Foreign Service only three years, Ms. Smedinghoff was helping to inaugurate a new school with U.S. assistance.

It is unfortunate that it takes tragic events like having an overseas mission stormed and U.S. envoys killed to bring to the public's attention that the work of their diplomats is anything but gutless or not serving the country well. The sacrifices of Ambassador Chris Stevens and his colleagues prove that all too well.

Embassy Attacks, Iran and Hollywood

I used to run into Richard Queen in the corridors of the State Department and chat. I saw his health deteriorate over the years from the effects of multiple sclerosis, his gait increasingly unsteady even with the aid of a cane. Richard was one of the fifty-two American diplomats taken hostage by Iranian militants in late 1979. He was twenty-eight then. A cheerful and pleasant fellow, Richard died of MS in 2002, at age fifty-one. Doctors speculated his hostage ordeal might have triggered the disease that killed him.

I had other friends who were at Embassy Tehran when it was seized. One, Lee Schatz, was in my junior officer trainee class. My first posting was Australia. His was Iran. Luck of the draw. Fortunately, Lee was one of the six diplomats who managed to evade capture and were exfiltrated from Iran in a joint Canadian-CIA operation, as dramatized in the movie, *Argo*. The fifty-two who weren't so lucky underwent 444 days of often barbaric treatment, ranging from beatings to mock firing squads and solitary. Another colleague, Mike

Metrinko, was beaten, kept in solitary for months and hand-cuffed 24/7 for two weeks straight when he dared to make critical comments about the Ayatollah Khomeni. After being freed, undaunted, Mike went on to serve twenty-seven more years of a distinguished Foreign Service career.

The wrenching Embassy Tehran takeover has had long lasting repercussions on the U.S. Foreign Service and other foreign affairs agencies. I saw them as a newly minted FSO. The outmoded strip paper shredders were replaced with disintegrators so that classified documents could not be pieced back together. The State Department strictly limited our holdings of classified material and improved the various ways of quickly destroying them. Greater stress was placed on security awareness. Those of us headed for danger posts were given training in evasive driving techniques and firearms. When Iran sent operatives out to plot attacks against American diplomats in the '80s, I was issued a weapon and provided 24/7 bodyguard coverage at the isolated consulate I headed. When I was harassed at the hostile posts where I served, the State Department came down on the host governments like a ton of bricks with diplomatic protests and threats to take other actions.

In the thirty-plus years since the Tehran embassy takeover, there have been twenty-five attacks against U.S. diplomatic missions, and ninety-six U.S. diplomats have lost their lives in the line of duty, four in the recent attack against our Benghazi consulate. I recently wrote about the Foreign Service being America's first line of defense, a fact lost on most Americans. Earlier, I'd described the rise of PTSD in the ranks of the Foreign Service – on a par with the rate experienced by military combat veterans. A buddy currently serving in Afghanistan just described for me his seven-day work week involving helicopter jaunts over Taliban territory to meet with his Afghan and NATO counterparts, trying to keep up with the ever increasing demand for yet more reports from a bloated embassy and five (yes, count 'em five) ambassadors; barely finding time to take a shower at his dust-infused outpost in the middle of nowhere.

In the inductee training Lee Schatz and I received, they told us that a U.S. diplomat's only armor is the Stars & Stripes, i.e., the American flag. Yes, U.S. Marine Security Guards protect 150 of over 285 diplomatic missions. And their primary mission is to "provide internal security. . .in order to prevent the compromise of classified material vital to the national security of the United States." In other words, they are not bodyguards, nor do they extend protective duties beyond a diplomatic post's walls. A diplomat is expected to jump into the middle of the local society and take his/her chances. The risks come with the territory, so to speak.

Argo is a ripsnorter of a thriller that will keep you white knuckled throughout its two-hour run. It's a "fictionalized account" of the drama that contributed to Pres. Carter's defeat for a second term. As such it has come under fire for shortshrifting or distorting the vital roles played by British, New Zealand, Swedish and Canadian diplomats in assisting their American colleagues. But the opening scenes of a growing mob storming the embassy and the utter defenselessness of the U.S. officials therein gives a goosebump-inducing realistic portrayal of diplomats under siege. The next time Congress plans to deprive the State Department of hundreds of millions of dollars for diplomatic security, our politicians would be wise to closely view *Argo*.

Iran Targets Foreign Diplomats: Beyond the Pale

The FBI and DEA exposed a bizarre plot by Iranian government entities to assassinate the Saudi ambassador in Washington. Taken straight out of a bad spy novel, the plot has the al-Quds unit of the Iranian Republican Guard recruiting a couple of Mexican drug cartel members to pull off the job with a purported payment of $1.5 million. Al-Quds allegedly did this via an Iranian-born American citizen, who reportedly has been spilling the beans to U.S. authorities about the whole scheme. This fellow made the mistake of recruiting two Mexican cartel members who also happened to be DEA informants. The two promptly informed their American handlers after being approached by the Iranians.

I was working on Lebanon and Palestinian issues in the State Department when Iran successfully carried through a scheme, through proxies, to blow up our Beirut embassy and the U.S. Marine barracks in 1983. Seventeen Americans were killed in the embassy bombing; 241 U.S. Marines were killed in the barracks attack. I was one of the people who debriefed our ambassador to Beirut right after the bombing. I also was the working-level officer in charge of coordinating our condemnation of the perpetrators in the United

Nations. A few years later, as head of a U.S. consulate in Thailand, I was given 24/7 bodyguard coverage and issued a weapon for a month in response to credible intelligence that Iran was targeting U.S. diplomats for assassination.

Iran's nefarious actions have a long track record. The regime in power there has been sponsoring terrorist actions for three decades. It is a regime that acts beyond the pale of civilized behavior and international law. In response, it has become increasingly isolated as the West has imposed more and more sanctions against it. Beyond public condemnations, additional sanctions are hard to come up with at this point. This is especially the case as Russia and China adamantly refuse to punish Tehran. Traditional friendship among rogues is one reason. Others include economic trade, oil and arms sales to the regime. Recent diplomatic efforts, however, may open a new chapter in Iran's relations with the rest of the world.

But a shadow conflict has been going on for years now between Western governments, along with Israel, and Tehran. An advanced and mysterious computer virus called Stuxnet set back Iran's nuclear program last year. Four Iranian nuclear scientists have also been assassinated in the past four years inside Iran; a fifth barely survived a bomb blast. One can surmise that the scheme to kill the Saudi ambassador in Washington is part of this bareknuckle battle behind the scenes, a retaliation perhaps.

Iran today is a complex and divided society with a government in turmoil, with the various leaders and their supporters vying against the others. At the same time, growing dissatisfaction with the Islamic regime occasionally manifests itself in public demonstrations. Yet the extreme Islamist elements continue to hold the upper hand. Until there is a "Persian Spring," the same extremist elements may well continue to hatch evil plots. That country's new leadership will need to reign these elements in if the new diplomacy is to work. Meanwhile, until the West is convinced Tehran is no longer seeking to devleop nuclear weapons, expect the shadow war to continue.

Diplomatic Asylum: Why an Embassy Isn't Embassy Suites

On November 4, 1956, Hungarian Cardinal József Mindszenty sought asylum in the U.S. embassy in Budapest as Soviet tanks invaded that country to restore communist leadership. Mindszenty didn't leave until 15 years later, following years of negotiations between Budapest, Washington and the Vatican.

On June 27, 1978, seven members of two Pentecostal families burst into the U.S. embassy in Moscow seeking asylum. They lived there in a cramped basement apartment until 1983 when they were allowed to return to their homes and await permission to emigrate.

On April 1, 1980, six Cubans crashed a bus through the Peruvian Embassy gates in Havana. After Peru refused to turn the asylum-seekers over to the Cuban government, Castro angrily ordered all security guards removed from the embassy perimeter whereupon more than 10,000 Cubans flooded onto the embassy grounds demanding asylum. After a two-week standoff, an agreement was reached to allow the people to leave the island.

On February 6, 2012, Chengdu police chief Wang Lijun entered the American consulate in that city, reportedly with a lot of dirt on the Bo Xilai case and possibly to seek asylum. Consulate officials managed to persuade the police chief to leave twenty-four hours later into the custody of central government reps.

In late April, Chinese dissident Chen Guangcheng escaped house arrest in his Shandong village and reportedly has found refuge in the U.S. embassy in Beijing. "Chen is under U.S. protection and high-level talks are currently under way between U.S. and Chinese officials regarding Chen's status," said a statement from the China Aid Association.

These are just a sampling of cases involving individuals seeking safety and asylum in foreign embassies. As can be seen, three of the cases entailed lengthy accommodation of the asylum-seekers inside embassies, even extending to years.

Diplomats' biggest fears when serving abroad are being the target of terrorists, taken hostage or assassinated. High on the list after these is having unwanted guests storm your diplomatic mission demanding protection from the host government. The reasons are: a) embassy/consulate security; b) political repercussions vis-a-vis the host government;

and c) major disruption in mission operations. Ideally, an ambassador and his/her staff aim to persuade the asylum-seeker(s) to leave the mission peacefully with assurances from the host government that it will take no retribution against them.

The Vienna Convention on Diplomatic Relations of 1961 stipulates that the premises of a diplomatic mission are inviolate and must not be entered by the host country except by permission of the head of the mission. The right to grant diplomatic asylum is not generally recognized by international law. U.S. embassies are authorized to grant temporary refuge for humanitarian reasons in extreme and exceptional circumstances, such as when the life or safety of the asylum-seeker is being threatened.

Having served in four communist countries, I have had first-hand experience with diplomatic asylum-seekers. In all but one case, we managed to persuade the asylum-seekers to return home quietly, sometimes with a commitment on our part to work constructively with the host government to help them emigrate or to be able to carry on their lives without retribution.

The exception involved a North Korean man who entered one of our embassies requesting political asylum. Our politically appointed non-career ambassador and his incompetent career Foreign Service deputy mishandled the case from the get-go. Without consulting embassy staff, they allowed the man to occupy a room inside our cramped building with no forethought as to what to do next. They then ordered all American staff to pull duty staying with the man 24/7. The man, of course, required food, medical attention, supplies – none of which was covered in standard budgeting. The embassy's security officer was beside himself with this decision to allow an uncleared individual – a national of an enemy state, no less – to reside indefinitely in the embassy. Embassy operations were being disrupted in a significant way. Many of us were unable to carry out our regular duties. The State Department threw the ball back in our court, telling us it was the ambassador's responsibility to resolve the case. Finally, I confronted the ambassador, laying out the written policies and guidelines governing such cases. The North Korean was an ordinary citizen of his country, having no intelligence value to us and no record as a dissident or a human rights activist. With the ambassador's go-ahead, I negotiated an arrangement whereby the U.N. refugee agency accepted the North Korean for resettlement in South Korea and the host government promised that it would not interfere. Case resolved, our embassy returned to what passed for normal.

There is nothing mystical or magical about an embassy. It is an office building like many others, only with perhaps more locks and security systems, and, in the case of the U.S., a detachment of Marine Guards. Otherwise, it is just a bunch of offices filled with standard office equipment, coffeemakers and desk photos of the wife or hubby and kids. In other words, it is not Embassy Suites. It is not designed to accommodate overnight guests. At the end of the day, the occupants go home to eat and sleep and goof off.

It would appear that the U.S. consulate in Chengdu handled the case of the police chief well, persuading him to leave and ensuring he was remanded into the hands of central government authorities instead of Bo Xilai's goons. As for the case of the human rights dissident Chen Guangcheng, U.S. Embassy Beijing had its work cut out for it and the case was resolved satisfactorily with Beijing allowing him to leave the country. The last thing our government would want would be to face a Cardinal Mindszenty scenario. In such a scenario, a diplomatic mission would need to get trained up by Embassy Suites in the hospitality business.

What the Foreign Service Can Learn from the U.S. Military

Pulitzer Prize-winning journalist Thomas Ricks's latest book, *The Generals*, is a fascinating study of U.S. Army military commanders from WWII to the present. It's an excellent evaluation of good vs. bad leadership. What particularly struck me were parallels to the Foreign Service and lessons that should be learned and applied. Following are highlights:

On Mediocrity
- An Army battalion commander said, "in today's Army, the B-minus and C-plus officer fares better than the A performer who occasionally takes risks and fails." "The personnel equivalent of Gresham's Law is that bad leaders drive out good ones."
- "A study in 2010 by the Army Reserve Institute concluded that 'the main reason talented people leave

is not the lure of a lucrative civilian career, but because mediocre people stay in and get promoted.'"

- "Success rarely can be rewarded adequately if failure carries little or no consequence. Nor will the standout officer be watched and imitated as he or she should be."

- Admiral Arleigh Burke said, "the first thing that a commander must learn is not to tolerate incompetence. As soon as you tolerate incompetence...you have an incompetent organization."

Keep the Outliers & Innovators

- "In considering 360's, it is also important that they do not reward the pleasant conformists and punish the brilliant outliers... All too often, an officer is promoted not for professional competence but... for being" a member of the club.

- Gen. George C. Marshall wrote, "There are very few of them, (who) are of that unusual type who enthuse all of their subordinates and carry through almost impossible tasks."

- There is a need "to keep alive the careers of outliers and innovators...so that they can be called upon during a crisis."

- In an article on leadership in the *Armed Forces Journal*, retired Army colonel Paul Yingling said, "in large organizations, the challenge is to keep the skeptics from becoming extinct."

- "Leadership should not be seen as a matter of officers taking turns or waiting in line."

- "We also should reward commanders who cultivate and maintain cultures in which their subordinates feel free to exercise initiative and speak their minds freely."

- Petraeus was fond of a company commander's sign put up in western Baghdad which said, "In absence of orders and guidance, figure out what they should have been and exercise vigorously."

On the Need to Be Able to Fire Incompetents

- "Relief then can be seen…not as a sign of the system failing but rather as a sign that the system is working."

- "When making such reliefs, it probably is better to announce them, in order to remove the mystery and dispel rumors… A relieved commander's peers need to be informed about why something has happened so they can learn from it."

- "Failure to relieve is sometimes a form of leadership indiscipline."

On Bureaucratic Resistance to Change

- A 2011 study by Harvard's School of Government found that most young Army officers left due to "limited ability to control their own careers" and "frustration with the military bureaucracy."

- "The former officers overwhelmingly believed that the Army did not reward talent with faster promotions and did not do a good job of matching talent to jobs." Among their recommendations: "Be willing to fire people for poor performance." Most valued talent in the Army: "don't rock the boat."

- "Any attempt to make such reforms will be attacked by the military bureaucracy." We should be wary when it "rejects suggested changes and defends current personnel policies on the grounds of 'fairness.'" This "puts the interests of the officers and bureaucracy above those of the rank and file and the nation as a whole."

Retired FSO, Jon P. Dorschner wrote about this need to take lessons from the U.S. military as well -- *Why the Foreign Service Should Be More Like the Army* -- in the June 2011 issue of the *Foreign Service Journal*. The son of an Army colonel and a former instructor at West Point, Mr. Dorschner addresses particularly the personal and moral side of things:

Importance of Esprit de Corps
- "I have never heard esprit de corps mentioned in the Foreign Service context. Instead, the Foreign Service emphasizes individuality over collegiality, exclusivity over inclusiveness. This is a hangover from its earlier history, when its membership was largely restricted to East Coast elites who were 'male, pale and Yale.'"

- "Yet class prejudices still linger and the Foreign Service often continues to connote elitism. What individual officers bring in the form of social class, elite education and family connections can still play a big role in placement and career advancement."

Primacy of Mission

- "The goal comes first and units are told to work cohesively to ensure successful completion of the mission. Individuals who showboat and subordinate the mission to their individual ambition do not do well and are singled out for correction. By contrast, the Foreign Service spends little or no time explaining to its members why they are doing what they are doing. Instead, duties are often performed mechanically. The mission becomes subordinate to the procedures. This is a common curse of bureaucratic organizations, and State Department bureaucracy is legendary."

- "Just as takes place in the Army, Foreign Service personnel should be told how their efforts fit into broader U.S. foreign policy and how their hard work and sacrifice benefit the nation. Otherwise, there is often no sense that a mission has been accomplished."

Need for Transparency

- "Foreign Service members who serve repeatedly in hardship posts are not provided a career advantage. Those who demonstrate dedication, hard work and technical expertise are not necessarily rewarded with regular promotions or choice assignments. This vagueness leads to accusations that 'it is not what you know but who you know,' and erodes morale."

Equal Treatment for All - Enforce the Rules

- "The State Department issues rules and then almost immediately makes exceptions to them. There are limits on how long personnel can serve in Washington, D.C. Those who do not serve in hardship posts are supposed to face negative consequences. Those who do not fulfill their language requirements are supposed to pay the price."

- "Like the military, we must staff positions in Iraq, Afghanistan and Pakistan that are dangerous and require separation from family. Everyone is supposed to pull their fair share, but for some reason it just doesn't happen. There always seem to be people who are able to manipulate the system. They stay in Washington longer than they are supposed to and avoid hardship tours, yet continue to be promoted."

- "A rule is a rule and must be enforced. Otherwise, the perception grows that the institution is not interested in fairness."

Controlling Egos

- "West Point cadets with large egos, who constantly tell their peers that they will become generals and who seek as much 'face time' as possible with

officers, are known as 'tools.' Being a tool is not a
good thing. This does not mean that the military
does not reward strong personalities, of course.
Ambition is the first requirement for anyone aspiring to make the higher grades, after all. But the
system teaches such individuals to rein in some of
that egoistic behavior."

- "West Point cadets learn that the most egotistical
  general is not always the most successful, and that
  an effective institution must make room for different leadership styles. Or, to put it another way: A
  little humility is not a bad thing. Perhaps the Foreign
  Service could benefit from a similar teaching model."

Looking After Subordinates' Interests
- "Officers and NCOs so egotistical and wrapped up
  in their own advancement that they do not show
  concern for the well-being of their subordinates receive poor evaluations and do not progress in their
  careers. From the outset, Army personnel are taught
  this essential component of leadership. By contrast,
  concern for subordinates is not part of the State
  Department evaluation process. Nor is there much
  emphasis on families. Instead, officers are taught
  to look after themselves and their careers first and
  foremost. This can lead, rightly or wrongly, to a
  perception by subordinates that 'successful' Foreign
  Service officers are those willing to do anything to
  get ahead, including letting down colleagues and
  disappointing subordinates."

- "These allegations arise out of the fact that such self-centered behavior is seldom punished in the Foreign Service. Selfishness and excessive egotism are not viewed as indicators of poor leadership and a lack of esprit de corps, but are often seen as the norm."

What are the chances that the USG and Department of State will pay heed and reform, adopting useful lessons from our military? Note the following:

"One of the worst abuses in the conduct of our foreign affairs is our habit of appointing 'lame ducks,' second-rate politicians and other incompetents, to important positions of international commissions or as delegates to international conferences. The other civilized nations as a rule appoint their government experts and diplomatic and consular representatives to these positions with the consequence that their representatives grow in wisdom and acquire a larger confidence and recognition from their fellow citizens."

~ *Recommendations for reforming the U.S. Foreign Service by the National Civil Service Reform League* - 1919.

Lawrence Eagleburger

Larry Eagleburger was a rare breed of diplomat. Stemming from a middle class German-American family in Milwaukee, he looked and acted like a regular guy, but had the fingerspitzgefuhl for human relations that only the very best of statesmen possess. He was a Kissinger acolyte which proved to be a vehicle for his outstanding talents both during and after his Foreign Service career.

On New Year's Eve, 1979, I was enroute by train from Milan to Belgrade to visit friends in our embassy there. Larry Eagleburger was the ambassador. While on the train, an Iraqi drugged my beverage, causing me to pass out for the better part of a day. The perp was never caught. A real Agatha Christie scenario. Italian police in Venice lodged me until I awoke the next day. The doctor who examined me couldn't make out what the Iraqi had put me out with, but deemed it a heavy, potentially life-threatening dose. U.S. Consulate staff put me on the next train to Belgrade.

Upon arrival, one of my friends informed me that the ambassador wished to see me immediately. In my first encounter with Eagleburger, I found him typically jacketless with his shirt sleeves rolled up. He queried as to my health and general state of being. When I told him the Iraqi had stolen my money, including travelers checks, Eagleburger reached into his pocket and pulled out a wad of U.S. dollars. "How much do you need?" he asked. I demurred, saying that I could certainly have money wired to me. Eagleburger then wasted no time calling the American Express rep in Belgrade and demanding that they restore my travelers checks immediately. The checks were delivered to the embassy that afternoon. He sent a cable to the U.S. ambassador in Rome and to the Department of State excoriating the U.S. Consul General in Venice for not having taken better care of a fellow FSO in trouble. Finally, he ordered his own staff to see to my well-being, requesting a status report later on.

This was classic Eagleburger. Hands-on, organized, caring. Years later, when I sat in on meetings Eagleburger had with senior foreign officials at the State Department, he always cut to the chase, briefing paper in one hand, cigarette in the other, telling his visitor like it was, interspersed with humor. He looked like a truck driver, talked like a Milwaukee pol but had the deftness of a surgeon. His staff loved him. And he rewarded them accordingly. If you worked hard and capably for him, Eagleburger personally ensured that you got a plum onward assignment and would even help you along further throughout your career. The loyalty was mutual.

When working as president of Kissinger Associates, Eagleburger would occasionally drive to meetings at the State Department in a flashy Corvette he termed his "Mid-life Crisismobile." He pulled himself out of the ridiculous auto supported by his cane and breathing heavily due to emphysema. This was the kind of colorful character we rarely witnessed at the gray, conformist headquarters building.

He was the only career FSO to have been Secretary of State, albeit only for forty-two days. He and we career people deserved a much longer term with Larry at the helm. But we who served under him are grateful for all that he gave and accomplished.

Moron-in-Chief

I'm not sure our State Department serves us well. I'm not talking about the Secretary of State here. I'm talking about the career diplomats and the Secretary of State, who all too often may not be making decisions or giving advice to the administration that's in this country's best interest. ~ Rick Perry.

The State Department is infested with communists. I have here in my hand a list of 205—a list of names that were made known to the Secretary of State as being members of the Communist Party and who nevertheless are still working and shaping policy in the State Department. ~ Sen. Joseph McCarthy.

My husband is in Iraq and hasn't seen me or our two daughters (2 years and 9 months) since June. Comments like Perry's make me want to cry in anger, frustration and sadness. ~ Katie (*Email "From the Embassy" blog*).

The United States has a rich history of demagoguery toward its diplomats. Through his alcohol-fueled lies, Sen. Joseph McCarthy laid waste to a whole generation of Foreign Service officers and stamped populist suspicion upon the entire U.S. State Department. His spiritual heir, Sen. Jesse Helms did more damage to our diplomatic establishment over the years he chaired the Senate Foreign Relations Committee than any combination of our foreign adversaries ever could have. And we had presidential candidate Rick Perry mindlessly espousing more calumny against our diplomats.

There are three underlying factors behind this diplomat-bashing by our politicians: (a) class warfare: a perception that the State Department is populated with liberal intellectual elitists; (b) xenophobia: a suspicion of all that is foreign and those who devote themselves to dealing with foreigners; and (c) a dismissiveness toward diplomacy in favor of military and intelligence solutions to vexing foreign problems.

Add to this, in Mr. Perry's case, a deep mistrust of government. This is the governor who judiciously advocated secession from the union. He's also the brilliant governor who didn't know the legal voting age in this country is eighteen. Perry's singling out career Foreign Service employees for his unsupported criticism was one in a long stream of attacks against the federal government he has made in his bumbling presidential campaign. They are cheap shots to stoke populist ire and support in this period of Tea Party-fed paranoia. Perhaps the third federal agency Mr. Perry failed to recall in his "brain-freeze" moment was the Department of State?

So, Mr. Perry, let's take just two recent examples of the Department of State giving bad advice to the President:

- The State Department's Intelligence and Research Bureau dissented from the conclusion in the National Intelligence Estimate on Iraq's WMD capabilities that Iraq was reconstituting its nuclear weapons program. "The activities we have detected do not…add up to a compelling case that Iraq is currently pursuing what INR would consider to be an integrated and comprehensive approach to acquiring nuclear weapons." State determined that the reports were "highly dubious."

- One month before the beginning of U.S. military operations in Iraq, the State Department warned of "serious planning gaps for post-conflict public security and humanitarian assistance." Recognizing that the military is reluctant "to take on 'policing' roles," the Department predicted that "a failure to address short-term public security and humanitarian assistance concerns could result in serious human rights abuses which would undermine an otherwise successful military campaign, and our reputation internationally."

And here's another thing to consider. One of the few benefits emanating from the Wikileaks affair is the universally high praise given to Foreign Service officers for their superior reporting, analysis and policy recommendations.

In the lobby of the State Department building are memorial plaques listing the names of 244 U.S. diplomats, including eight ambassadors, who gave their lives in the line of duty, people who dedicated themselves to providing sound information and advice to their president. Flippant remarks like yours, governor, dishonor our envoys who gave their full measure to their country. And they belittle the sacrifices Foreign Service family members like Katie and her daughters endure.

So, Mr. Perry, you have demonstrated almost on a daily basis, through your repeated gaffes and severe BDS (brain deficit syndrome) that you are not ready for prime time, that with you as president, it would be curtains for this country.

As they say in Texas, "An empty bucket makes the most racket." And you, sir, are a case in point.

Ask Not...

"Which College Grads Snag the Best Salaries?"
— *CNNMoney.com*

"Highest-Paid Bachelor's Degrees: 2011" – *CNBC*

"Ten Highest Paying Career Paths" – *Collegecrunch.com*

"Top-Paying Entry-Level Jobs For College Grads"
— *Forbes Magazine*

"Government is not the solution to our problem; government is the problem." – *Pres. Ronald Reagan*

"Ask not what your country can do for you. Ask what you can do for your country." – *Pres. John F. Kennedy*

"It is for us the living, rather, to be dedicated here to the unfinished work which they who fought here have thus far so nobly advanced." – Pres. *Abraham Lincoln*

Each month *State Magazine*, the official employees journal of the Department of State arrives in the mail. I peruse retirements and the obits and then toss it. From the beginning of my career up to the present time, I've always been struck by death notices like the following, which I culled from a couple of recent issues:

- Adele E. Davis, died Dec.4. "She served in the Navy WAVES during WWII" and "assisted her (FSO) husband during postings to Laos, Hong Kong, Haiti, Turkey, South Arabia, Greece and Jamaica."
- Ralph H. Cadeaux, 84, died Nov. 29. "A Marine veteran wounded on Iwo Jima," he joined the Foreign Service in 1954 and served in Italy, Africa, Vietnam, UK and Israel.
- Edward W. Holmes, 87, died Dec. 18. "He served in the Army during WWII and joined the Foreign Service in 1946."
- Roman Leo Lotsberg, 84, died Oct. 27. "He served in the Army Air Force during WWII" He served as an FSO in Vietnam, Morocco, India, France, Egypt, Greece, Iran.
- William Keller Miller, 90, died Jan. 1. "Following service in the Army Air Corps in WWII, he joined the Foreign Service in 1951" and served in India, Finland, Taiwan, Switzerland and the UK.
- Norman Edwin Barth, 83, died Nov. 15. "He served in the Army during WWII and joined the Department in 1957."
- R. Richard Runbottom, Jr., 98, died Dec. 6. "He was in the Navy during WWII and then joined the Department where he served often in Latin America and Spain."

There is a consistent pattern to these departed members of the Greatest Generation. They fought in WWII and then, often after a multi-year hiatus, returned to public service in the international arena. Their wartime military experience obviously instilled in them a sense of serving the greater good as well as a sense of the larger world out there. They got the itch. The obits of the '70s through the '90s were especially fascinating given the bygone diplomatic postings where many had served: "American Legation Tangier," "U.S. High Commission in Germany," "U.S. Mission, Godthaab, Greenland," "American Embassy Chungking," "U.S. Consulate Liverpool."

The ranks of these retired octo- and nonagenarians are fast dwindling and their fascinating lives will soon all fade into history. It is especially sad because they were of an idealistic generation. Graduates of America's best universities, they forewent big-salaried private sector jobs for government careers to promote American ideals and objectives in a world war and the bitter cold war that followed.

Another generation that was driven by American ideals was that which came of age during the Kennedy administration. Many U.S. diplomats started out as Peace Corps volunteers, drawn to public service by JFK's inaugural "Ask not..." speech. I was a child when Kennedy died, but his idealism, progressivism and call to service resonated in my head and I knew from an early age the path I would follow in life.

In contrast to these previous eras, there is an ugly spirit in the land today, one of self-centeredness, greed and contempt for public service. It has brought with it near collapse of our economy, growing intolerance and a widening gulf in the political discourse. What is most disturbing is the open talk of violence among even elected officials. As can be seen from the headlines leading this essay, the media focus on young people in college centers on the pursuit of money. Scanning the press, I have seen no call to the high-minded values enunciated by JFK and his predecessors, except by Barack Obama when he was campaigning to be president. I find this sad and disturbing. Youth should be synonymous with idealism. America was founded on that principle as a core element of our democracy. Its absence from our national psyche early in this new century bodes ill for our future as the Founding Fathers' ideals take a back seat to xenophobia, narcissism and avarice. One can only hope that a return to "the better angels of our nature" will be forthcoming. The burden lies on an idealistic youth to spearhead it.

Life After the Foreign Service, Part I

Our clueless ambassador in a war-torn country where guerrillas were targeting and killing foreigners ordered his embassy staff to travel into the lawless interior to monitor people's attitudes toward UN-sponsored free elections, an order which the staff defied. My wife experienced a complicated and life-threatening pregnancy after MED – the State Department's medical unit – refused to authorize business class travel to the destination where she would give birth. My boss in a communist country violated security rules in his emails, resulting in the host government's harassment of one of our best sources. The promotion and assignments processes were becoming an even more uneven playing field. ...Time to leave the Foreign Service.

There is nothing like a Foreign Service career: getting paid to travel the world and live in foreign countries representing one's country; dealing with Big Picture issues; working with some of the smartest people on the planet; a variety in work content virtually unmatched in any other career. Twenty-three years in the U.S. Foreign Service gave me no end of challenges and adventures and opportunity to apply my brainpower toward history-making events and to meet presidents, kings and high-caliber intellectuals. I had the time of my life. But too many shortcomings in the system compelled me to make the decision to leave my government career early and to find reward in greener pastures.

As one advances in the ranks, one hears the refrain, "Is there life after the Foreign Service?" – accompanied by much wringing of the hands. Contemplating the end of one's diplomatic career is akin to those 15th century folk who saw monsters and oblivion at the edge of world's end. It's understandable. After decades of working in a profession, what else does one know? And how do you apply airy-fairy statecraft skills to making money on the outside? Many turn to academia, think tanks, independent consulting, NGOs and international organizations. Logical fits.

Sorry. Not for this free spirit. Determined, against the counsel of family and friends, never to hold down another job again, never again to don suit and tie for work, never again to answer to a boss, never again to commute to an office, I made the wild and crazy decision to return to my roots: work on the family farm. Oops! Nope! The family farm was sold years ago. I mean my later roots: being a writer and making a living off of it. I turned down a lovely offer from a college president to be a "diplomat-in-residence," teaching a couple of courses and assisting in setting up a nascent international relations program. Then I declined a nice offer from a London-based political consulting company to take on assignments from them. The reason? I was too preoccupied with selling my spy-mob thriller, *Permanent Interests* and my war criminal thriller, *CHASM*. And my literary agent was expecting much more of me after the 2011 release of my Afghanistan thriller, *Tribe*. Teaching college and political consulting, simply put, would interfere in the marketing of my twisted fantasies.

Rather than doing the "right thing," this ex-FSO decided to follow his dream: fiction writing. I sit in my armchair at home or in my favorite cafe dreaming up and writing down plots involving Machiavellian politicians, lustful doyennes, mad generals, ruthless spies, flawed heroes and world-threatening events – drawing from my rich motherlode of Foreign Service experiences.

And it's worked! All three of my thrillers and have been Amazon bestsellers, topping the lists for Political Fiction, Spy Stories and Action & Adventure. My agent also represents Stieg Larsson (*The Girl With the Dragon Tattoo*, etc). I've received positive blurbs and reviews from *NYT* bestselling authors and have been featured on NBC's *Today*

Show, *The Washington Post*, *Christian Science Monitor*, SiriusXM Radio, *Huffington Post* and other media. Nice exposure for selling more books. I'm actually making a living doing this. Of course, it ain't easy when you lack full first amendment rights (see *Why I'm Censored*).

The lesson? "Do the right thing" doesn't necessarily apply. You've done that for years as a buttoned-down, team-playing, don't-rock-the-boat bureaucrat. Try something new. Listen to your heart and follow your dreams. I did.

Life After the Foreign Service, Part II

> Clusiot: *You're Louis Dega. I'm Clusiot.*
> *How come you ended up in a place like this?*
>
> Dega: *Patriotism.*
>
> ~ *Papillon* (movie, 1973)

Nary a week goes by that I don't find among the Key Search Words of my blog stats variations on the following:

"life after the foreign service"
"careers after the foreign service"
"deciding to leave the foreign service"
"leaving the foreign service"

A sizable segment of my reading audience comprises U.S. Foreign Service personnel. Many of these are actively contemplating leaving the service, but are anxious about timing, life plans and post-partum depression. Some Foreign Service folks are on the threshold of retirement. Others of you are unhappy and simply wish to turn a new leaf, finally make an honest living. Still others have personal reasons ranging from relationship commitments to health issues to children's needs, etc. In *Life After the Foreign Service*, I said, "'Do the right thing' doesn't necessarily apply. You've done that for years as a buttoned-down, team-playing, don't-rock-the-boat bureaucrat. Try something new. Listen to your heart and follow your dreams. I did." This is clearly easier said than done. Being a cautious, rick-averse sort, with two toddlers and a foreign-born wife, I chose a decade ago to give up a government salary for a secure career in fiction writing. Next, with the help of some friends, I plan to break into Hollywood, also a no-brainer. The Foreign Service prepared me well for these pursuits, with Daliesque career turns, personalities straight out of *One Flew Over of the Cuckoo's Nest*, Kafkaesque bureaucracy, and a personnel system that could keep Rod Serling at his typewriter for decades. My leap has yielded success with three Kindle bestsellers, national media attention and selected among the top twenty percent out of 10,000 entrants in the Amazon Breakthrough Novel Award contest with my fourth novel. Yes, next stop, Hollywood.

Camp Commandant: *Make the best of what we offer you, and you will suffer less than you deserve.*

For those of you who feel trapped on a bureaucratic Devil's Island and with the desperate need to escape, you may wish to be bolder than I: take that leap into becoming a trapeze artist with Cirque du Soleil, a male stripper, or starring in your very own nationally syndicated cooking show. But if you're a hopeless prisoner of the nothing-ventured-nothing-lost

Foreign Service culture, go for those lucrative UN consulting jobs, diplomat-in-residence teaching posts, or processing FOIA requests in the basement of SA-137½. Foreign
Service people have a wealth of training and experiences
to draw on to take the next leap into the private sector or
other areas. I think many may undervalue the transferabil-
ity of their skills. This is a possible shortcoming that each
individual must overcome. I chose to take the unusual step
of following my passion for creative writing. I did not want
a "paycheck job," and eschewed forever bosses, commutes,
dress codes and office politics. Others are comfortable in
that world. If you are, go for it. But, if, like me, you're not,
don't tie your hands.

Dega: *If I stay - here in this place - I will die!*

While serving as Chargé d'Affaires in Phnom Penh in the
early '90s, I had the mixed fortune of hosting Richard
Holbrooke for a weekend. Bored in the private sector,
Mr. Holbrooke was angling for a position in the Clinton
administration, so went on a "fact-finding" jaunt to Southeast Asia. But that's another story. Anyway, the garrulous
former FSO leaned forward while we were having drinks
one evening, locked his eyes on mine, pointed his index finger at me and said, "The Foreign Service will always break
your heart." (In his Scarsdale accent, he said, "haht.") I'm
sure he had his own career path in mind when he said this,
having quit the service after a decade to pursue a meteoric
rise in foreign affairs by way of journalism, business and
government.

I knew too many colleagues at State who were locked in bitter resentment in a career they no longer enjoyed. Their corrosive attitude wore on the rest of us, sometimes hindering the goals we needed to accomplish. They stayed in out of the need to pay the bills, reach that twenty years to be able to retire early, or the simple lack of courage and imagination to take the leap. I felt sorry for most of these people and occasionally tried to counsel them friend-to-friend. Others, with an inborn malignant streak, I ignored. If you detest what you're doing, but feel trapped, weigh the toll it may be taking on your health -- mental as well as physical -- and on your relationships with your loved ones. And while I greatly appreciate your reading my essays -- really! -- I don't want to write any more "Life After" essays. And you will find the answers not in cyberspace, but in your own heart.

Maybe the past is like an anchor holding us back. Maybe, you have to let go of who you were to become who you will be.
~ Carrie Bradshaw, *Sex And The City*

So, if your passion is trapeze, stripping, or cooking, and you're either leaving the service, or desperately wanting to leave, focus on the possibilities more than the hindrances. Everybody I knew thought I was nuts (some still do!) for not taking a safey post-FS route, having turned down a college teaching position, a consulting job, gigs teaching regional studies to spooks, and stiffing Mother State on WAE assignments. Call me crazy. Meanwhile, I collect royalties. And then there's Hollywood…

Miles: *Joel, you wanna know something? Every now and then say, "What the f---." "What the f---" gives you freedom. Freedom brings opportunity. Opportunity makes your future.*
~ Risky Business (movie 1983)

Yes, Virginia, There Really is a U.S. Department of State

At a friend's party not long ago, a woman I'd never met came up to me and started a conversation. "So, what did you do before becoming a writer?" she asked. I said I'd worked for the U.S. State Department as a Foreign Service officer for twenty-three years. The woman giggled, rolled her eyes and retorted, "Oh! We all know what that means. You were a spy." My stone-faced demeanor reflected my displeasure with this woman's insensitive and moronic statement.

Like most of my colleagues, I've experienced this type of encounter countless times both during my Foreign Service career and after. I used to disabuse the irresponsible lame-brains who made the allegation, which they usually did in a loud voice so all within shouting distance could hear. Over time, however, I decided to go on counterattack. Not long after making friends in the small rural village where we now live, another transplant -- a former Hollywood screenwriter -- at social get-togethers repeatedly cracked, "We all know where you really worked. Ha. Ha." And another fellow, a journalist, would snicker, "Yep. CIA. We all know. Tee hee." After this occurred two or three times, I launched my counterattack: "'Hollywood screenwriter' and 'journalist,' eh? Don't try to hide it. Everybody knows you worked in the pornography business." Then I'd repeat the charge in a louder non-jocular tone so the whole room could hear. This proved to be the right antidote. Later, the three of us cleared the air. I'd stop publicly smearing them as pornographers if they ceased their lame insinuations about me having been a spook. I also counseled them as to the dangers of pinning such a label on USG employees, active duty or retired. Being slapped with the label of intelligence officer could lead to physical threats against the recipient, especially when traveling abroad. My friends have been circumspect ever since.

But this leads to a broader perception problem. Most Americans don't seem to be aware that their country has its very own foreign ministry, and that we call it the Department of State. They may be aware of Secretary Hillary Clinton and a handful of her predecessors from watching the news, but beyond that haven't a clue as to what State does. My late mother would shake her head in incomprehension whenever I tried to explain my profession as a diplomat. And this cluelessness was shared by many other family members and friends who lived outside the D.C. beltway. I would be reduced to saying "I deal with foreign countries" and leave it at that. Of course, the rejoinder often was, "So, you're a spy then."

Much of the blame for this mass ignorance can be laid on Hollywood. The Bourne series, James Bond, Mission Impossible, *Homeland* and countless other movies and TV series about spies and espionage have long captured the public's imagination, as have military dramas. This goes as well for the thriller novels upon which many of these movies are based. How many movies have been made involving diplomats as action figures? If a movie or book thriller has any diplomats at all in its plot, they're more often than not portrayed as sniveling, effete cowards out to foil brave spies or soldiers with their backroom machinations. Even the recent hit movie, *Argo*, essentially depicted American diplomatic hostages in Iran as passively awaiting rescue by the bold, brave CIA exfiltration officer.

This lack of awareness and respect for our diplomatic service has incurred serious harm. Sen. Joseph McCarthy led a crusade to destroy the Foreign Service based on scurrilous lies. He was partly successful, having singlehandedly wrecked the careers of the post-WWII China Hands. Years later, Sen. Jesse Helms picked up the mantle of ill-will by slashing our foreign affairs budget, UN contributions and rejecting or delaying the appointments of many Foreign Service officers to higher positions. Americans allowed these demagogues to get away with their vindictive attacks against the State Department, in part, because of their own ignorance. If Schwarzenegger or Cruise or Damon had played hero-diplomat roles, perhaps attacks from the political right might have been blunted. Alas, those who wage war or steal official secrets make for more interesting fiction than do peacemakers.

So, diplomats, go on the counterattack. Next time that human resources factotum from Widgets, Inc. sniggers that you're a spy, fire back in a loud voice that he's the first human trafficker you've ever met. Or when your local pharmacist sneers about your real vocation as an intel spook, fire back that his being a drug dealer must get him in trouble with the law a lot. Use your imagination. Put yourself in the shoes of another action figure, Dirty Harry, and say, *Make my day!*

Confessions of a Sleeper Agent

Just after we'd settled in the small rural village (pop. 2600) in which we now reside, the rumors began flying. The first, predictable, one was, "He's a CIA agent working under-cover." That one got some traction and for years I've found imaginative ways to shoot it down. Forget about why the CIA would plunk one of its "agents" in Toad Stool Hol-low, USA. I took particular delight, however, in the second rumor: "They're in the FBI's witness protection program." I relished the notoriety I got from this rumor. But how many Ivy League-educated introverts of farmer stock get mistaken for mafiosi? I didn't care. I went out of my way to stoke this rumor, including trying to affect a Brooklyn accent and a facial twitch. Why the rumors? Because the American hinterland simply has a hard time processing "he's an American diplomat-turned-writer with a Dutch wife whose kids were born in South Africa and who are all multilingual."

Over dinner the other day, I told my wife, "You know, I feel like one of those Russian sleeper agents." She expressed puzzlement. "Yeah," I said. "I live an identity that isn't my own, participate in a way of life that doesn't come naturally and must affect a down-home patter whenever I mingle with the locals." As with most of my off-the-cuff commentary, she dismissed it as crazy talk. That's why I didn't continue with comparing us with the old *Saturday Night Live* TV comedy Conehead family, outer space aliens stranded in American suburbia after their spaceship had crashed on earth.

But, continuing with the "illegals" formula, let's look at some examples. Days after moving in, I stopped in my tracks while walking down Main St. and began laughing like a mad man. Why? A sign in a hair salon window proclaimed, "Walk-ins Welcome!" In my world, "walk-ins" were defectors who appeared unannounced at an embassy requesting political asylum. During my strolls or while driving, I found myself inadvertently conducting surveillance detection runs. I stopped at storefront windows to view reflections of a possible "tail" and double tracked, memorizing faces, again, to detect a tail. One eye was always in the rearview mirror. My phone conversations were guarded and terse, used as I was to electronic bugging. I turned the radio up loud when conducting private conversations. My trained ear would try to discern AK rounds in holiday fireworks. I applied my Kremlinology skills in analyzing local power structures. Big mistake. The mayor is not an appointed apparatchik and you cannot consider PTA members as conniving politburo aspirants each with his or her own power base. The village court is not rigged and dialectical materialism is worth less than the grocery list. No, the Girl Scouts are not a front organization; it's okay for your daughters to join. The school board does not conduct purges. Not usually anyway.

At social get-togethers, in response to the inevitable question, "So what do you do?" I respond, "I'm a writer. I worked previously for the U.S. State Department." "Ah. State Department, huh? So, how long did you live in Albany?" Then the rumors begin. "Psst. They're like Brad Pitt and Angelina Jolie in that movie, Mr. & Mrs. Smith"). Of course, what can you expect when you're called out of the blue by a State Department bureaucrat coolly advising you to pack your bags for return to active duty to Afghanistan? Or, the fact that you write bestselling spy novels that must be security reviewed by government censors? Or, that you tool around in a '72 U.S. Army jeep you brought back from Vietnam? These are not exactly the quotidian activities of butchers, bakers and candlestick makers. Having spent the bulk of my government career in or tracking communist regimes, guerrilla movements, puppet states, satrapies, dictatorships and the byzantine U.S. foreign affairs bureaucracy has left me a twisted soul, largely out of touch with my own society, a sleeper agent in my adopted home town. Excuse me. My handlers are expecting me at a dead drop location and some State Department functionary is calling…

Greta Garbo & Me

I want to be left alone. ~ Greta Garbo

I turned down a gracious offer to be a paid consultant by a new London-based political consultancy firm. Not long ago, I declined a generous offer from a college president to become "Diplomat-in-Residence" entailing teaching and managing a new international relations program. Not long after that, educational contractors of a super-secret government agency invited me to teach short courses to their staff. I took a pass. The U.S. State Department asked me to fill out papers to reactivate my top secret security clearances so that they could call me back to serve in either Iraq or Afghanistan. Those forms gather dust on a shelf. State pointedly informed me that they could call me up anyway at any time. "Make my day," I retorted. This faustian-mephistophelean parrying with my erstwhile employer began when I signed my soul away to Uncle Sam many years ago.

A diplomatic career is a very social one. A diplomat's job entails constantly cultivating contacts and giving and attending all manner of dinners, receptions and parties. One also sometimes finds oneself covered by the news media. A diplomat lives in a fish bowl. It's a wonderful career for extroverts, but can be draining for introverts. I fall into the latter category.

When I hung up my cummerbund a decade ago, I made an oath to myself never to hold down a "job" ever again. No more suits and ties (with the exception of funerals), no more bosses, no more office politics, no more commuting. My family and friends, naturally, think me nuts. But, like Greta, whom the public also thought slightly cuckoo, I want to be left alone, to write tales of adventure, intrigue, romance and madness – in solitary. Like a diplomat, I want to be paid to lie, but I want to do so on my own terms.

So, I ponder the remote, mysterious and beautiful Greta Garbo, who retired from the movies at age thirty-six to "be left alone." Her allure nonetheless endured over the decades. I myself have no such illusions. As a burnt-out government functionary-turned-hack fiction writer, I'm satisfied with my chosen path. So, while I am flattered by your offers to re-employ me, please leave me alone…

…though the right amount of flattery and money possibly could make me reconsider.

SEX AND FOREIGN "AFFAIRS"

Love, Romance and Sex in the U.S. Foreign Service - Part I: Of Lust & Loneliness

Never play cards with a man named 'Doc.'
Never eat at a place called 'Mom's.'
And never sleep with someone who has troubles worse than your own.

Diplomats have a justifiable reputation for being impeccably proper, bloodless figures whose passions get stirred by a good concerto, a stimulating dinner party, a good book. But diplomats are human too. After all, they do procreate just like real people; though, perhaps they have fewer progeny.

The U.S. State Department has a well-deserved reputation for being manned by people who are morally irreproachable, temperamentally self-controlled and emotionally repressed. It is reflected in the cascade of grays and blues one observes in Foggy Bottom attire, the orthodox hair styling, the faces that don't register easily in one's memory. Family values of a progressive bent pervade the culture. Conformity is the creed. Norman Rockwell on steroids. Like nonconforming meerkats, the wild in behavior, the over-the-top eccentrics, the loners, the terminally weak, the wildcatters, the truly innovative and those who are too New York menschlich are either driven off the reservation or insidiously sidelined until their career comes to a premature end.

But sex is a fact of life. And, like it or not, Foreign Service folk can't escape it. The peccadilloes keep State's security cadre very busy indeed. First, let's categorize the broad rubrics of sexual behavior in the American Foreign Service:

Midlife Adolescence: the married middle-aged male who suddenly finds himself in a sexual playground like Bangkok or Manila and loses it.

The Poor Soul: the man or woman whom love has passed by and plunges into a marriage with a Third Worlder who recognizes a free ticket out of misery when s/he sees it.

The Political Appointee Who Mistakes 'Diplomatic Immunity' for Diplomatic Impunity: When to mischief we bend our will, how soon we find the instruments of ill.

The Gays: (a) those open about their sexuality (tending to be younger), and (b) those firmly in the closet (tending to be older).

Sleeping With the Enemy: violators of the "non-frat" policy who have affairs with the nationals of hostile powers.

The Nut Cases: exhibitionists, predators, the morally unhinged.

Middle-aged Adolescents: While in diplomatic train-ing after just entering the Foreign Service, a middle-aged woman offered me a ride home from the Foreign Service Institute in her van with three young children. She had just returned from Bangkok where her husband was posted. "Oh, Bangkok. That must be very interesting," I said, mak-ing conversation. She harrumphed. "I couldn't wait to get out of there," she said. She went on to relate how, after a few months at post, her husband took up with an assort-ment of Thai bar girls and abruptly ended their marriage. She came home with their kids to pick up the pieces of her life and deal with lawyers and State Department bureaucrats on the red tape surrounding divorce. Even one of our mar-ried career ambassadors carried on with local honies. The Thai have a strong sense of joie de vivre about such things, but most Americans don't want Hugh Hefner representing their country overseas.

And there was the notorious case of a colleague who was sent packing from another Asian post because he had decided to divorce his generic American wife for a young Chinese woman with whom he had fathered babies. But the wife hung on and both women lived with him at the same time. This harem chief confided that what ticked him off was that the ambassador who made him depart was himself living with a local mistress.

It's a sad yet all too familiar tale. Middle-aged men tossed into overseas sexual playgrounds where any Western gentle-man is a catch by dint of his income and passport. I lost count early on as to how many male colleagues I knew who dumped June Cleaver for Suzie Wong. There's something about women raised in traditional societies who know how to serve their men. They exhibit no pretense of gender equality, spend loads of time in the kitchen cooking up spicy curries, are often good in bed and just don't complain too much. Some were indeed bar girls. Others, however, were middle or upper class in their native countries. In my experience, most are smarter and sharper than the Caspar Milquetoasts they marry. Love is not so important to them as is security. And, though they pamper their men, they usually are the ones who call the shots.

A place like Thailand is great for self-deluded studs, but a hellhole for foreign women. Frustrated in love, many of the latter hit on the available bachelors within the embassy community. Being the target of such approaches over the years by both married and single Western ladies, I speak from personal experience.

The Poor Soul: How often one encounters the frumpy plain Jane with her new hubby – an Ethiopian rock star half her age, the Paul Giamatti look-alike wed to buxom 22-year old Miss Ukraine. I recall the forty-something Foreign Service secretary who married a tattooed Fijian Hell's Angels Harley aficionado. A match made in heaven. The face-in-the-crowd mid-life consul, trained as a classical pianist, biggest suck-up in the Service, who fell deeply in love with a smashing young college-educated Korean girl. Like teen love birds, they were. Until she got her American passport. The first thing Miss Korean Beauty did upon landing at LAX was to file divorce papers. Another common scenario.

You see, foreign spouses are entitled to almost instant U.S. citizenship upon marrying an American diplomat. Too many have discovered this Get Out of Teeming Developing World Free card. The ones with a trace of moral conscience might wait a year or two before ditching Mr. or Ms. Meal Ticket. Others, like the Korean babe, have it all scammed out and ditch their new mate as soon as the ink is dry on their shiny new eagle-embossed passport.

Political Appointees: Someone needs to collect 200-years of lore and write a book about the idiots who are allowed to buy United States ambassadorships. No banana republic rivals our diplomatic spoils system, a topic to which I plan to devote a special entry soon. But here are just two examples of political appointee ambassadors who were caught in sexual misconduct:

Former U.S. Ambassador to Norway Mark Evans Austad, an outspoken former Mormon missionary who hurled verbal attacks against a variety of Norwegian liberal institutions as well as the press was taken by police at a house where he was bellowing loudly and banging on a woman's door at 3 a.m. Austad claimed that, after hosting a cocktail party, he headed to a friend's house "to plan a salmon fishing trip," and the taxi had taken him to the wrong address. The police returned Austad to his residence.

Joseph Zappala, a wealthy Florida developer and fundraiser for President George H.W. Bush, was appointed ambassador to Spain despite his inability to speak Spanish. Zappala's tour in Madrid was marred when he took up with another woman, ending his thirty-year marriage. "This guy's roaming eye for the Spanish ladies became very embarrassing for us in the career Foreign Service," said someone who served in Madrid with Zappala.

Gays: A senior protocol official was nabbed in a raid on a Washington gay brothel years ago. He faced a dual dilemma at that time: the shame and security implications of being outed as gay when it was not condoned, and the legal issues of being arrested as a john in a pay-for-sex situation.

Prior to the 1990s, homosexuality was grounds for exclusion from the Foreign Service. Enforcement, however, was spotty at best. Everybody had friends and colleagues known to be gay. It was no big deal. But the gays themselves were forced to remain in the closet. When the ban was lifted, gays organized themselves into their own Gays and Lesbians in Foreign Affairs Agencies. While younger FS members are open about their gayness, many of the older ones remain closeted, whether out of habit or whatever. The bottom line is the Foreign Service is a much friendlier institution for gays than in previous years, particularly since Secretary Clinton initiated some reforms to accommodate partners.

Sleeping With the Enemy: the national security agencies have what is called a "Criteria Countries List" comprising those nations whose intelligence services target our personnel (see "On Spies, Counterspies, Would-be Spies and Just Plain Losers - Part I"). A "non-frat" policy applies. Think: Russia, China, Cuba, Iran, etc. It is verboten to have romantic relationships with the citizens of such countries. Nonetheless…

There was the junior FSO who fell in love with an East German woman while posted in another communist country. The young female FSO who had a torrid romance with a Cuban man while serving in Havana. The embassy communicator who up and married another country's army officer while serving at a communist post. Diplomatic Security pulled their clearances, yanked them from their postings and placed them in dead-end nonprofessional jobs back in D.C. At least two were assigned to the Department's mail room. They got the message and quit. BTW, the guy with the East German lady and the woman who married the foreign officer enjoyed happy marriages outside of the Foreign Service.

Nut Cases: There was the USAID official who had a penchant for displaying his private parts to females who entered his office (yes, he was dismissed). And the admin staff sleazebag in one of our large embassies who coerced his local national female employees into sex acts with him in his office (got off scot-free; an all-too familiar crime in our embassies). The married, sixtyish political appointee Under Secretary of State who preyed sexually upon his female secretary (who filed a grievance action leading to his quiet dismissal). And there is at least one confirmed case of incest.

The U.S. Foreign Service consists of America's best in terms of brains, abilities and relevant knowledge. But its members are all too human just like the rest of us. No, Foreign Service personnel are not a bunch of kinky perverts lusting after the people with whom they work and associate. But funny things do happen in life. And the system is pretty good about policing itself. Messy adulterous affairs overseas often end up with the involved parties being sent back home, with a cloud over their careers. Our diplomats are held to high standards which are taken seriously.

I incorporate sexual escapades as described herein in my novels about the American power set and their many fallibilities. As you can see, you can't make this stuff up.

Love, Romance and Sex in the U.S. Foreign Service - Part II: Bombs & Bureaucrats

The love of one's country is a splendid thing.
But why should love stop at the border? ~ Pablo Casals

<u>**Six Tips on Courtship in a War Zone**</u> *(Cosmo Mag – are you paying attention?)*

When your love interest calls via military radio phone from a jungle redoubt asking for advice on what to do as mortar rounds slam into her encampment, counsel her as follows: "Hit the ground!"

When dating via helicopter over enemy terrain, become a Believer and pray to God often – even if you aren't a Believer, it's best to hedge your bets when your life is on the line.

24/7 armed guards who accompany you wherever you go can put a crimp on your dating as well as the rest of your social life. Stay at home until the danger passes.

Kevlar trumps Ralph Lauren and Dolce & Gabbana: don't fret about making a fashion statement in a place where olive drab dominates the runways. There's something to be said about bullet-stopping Kevlar even if it does suppress the fine lines of your figure.

When the local fare moves on your plate, or all those around you are retching their guts out, a dinner date centered on Meals-Ready-to-Eat (MREs) is an acceptable fallback.

When traveling over jungle cover in which wild-eyed, drug-crazed freedom fighters love to take pot shots at low-flying aircraft just for the hell of it, do anything possible to protect your private parts, as these may come in handy as your romance progresses to the next stage. Helmets, flak jackets and medical kits are just some of the items you can use for this purpose.

Is This a Date, or Apocalypse Now?

A fetching young Dutch UN peacekeeper caught my eye when I was serving at our new embassy in war-torn Cambodia in the early '90s. There was something about the blue beret, the gouda-infused enthusiasm to bring Freedom and Democracy to the benighted Cambodians, her sacrificing her wooden shoes for jungle boots, her patriotic profile in a black one-piece swimsuit at the only pool in the country.

We hit it off. Then she was posted to the country's far north-east, an area so remote that no roads led to it, a backwater in which we stumbled upon anti-communist Vietnamese guerrillas who didn't know Hanoi had won in '75, a region dominated by exotic minority peoples speaking languages unknown to linguists, an ecological wonderland with animal species thought to be extinct. The only way to get there was by chopper. The UN contracted transportation out to a Russian company operating rickety Soviet-era helicopters piloted by Red Army veterans, many of whom made their bones in Afghanistan. It wasn't unusual for Khmer Rouge guerrillas to shoot at these choppers; bullet holes occasionally were found in the fuselages after landing.

When in D.C. on a date, one needs only to hop into one's shiny new Miata, pick up one's date and zip over to Marcel's for filet of Dorade and foie gras mousse, to be followed by drinks at Veritas and maybe a late showing of Woody Allen's latest. When dating in Stung Treng, however, one must lower one's standards a notch or two. With alcohol-sodden, joyriding Russians at the stick, I flew too many times than I care to remember between Phnom Penh and Stung Treng. I got a break when our own POW/MIA search team flew Blackhawks to that region to excavate the remains of our Vietnam War missing-in-action. Otherwise, we kept in touch via Australian military radiophone. Indeed, she did call me one afternoon asking what to do as mortar rounds fell into her encampment (I could hear the explosions over the receiver). And I shouted, "Hit the ground!"

Mother State

Something like sixty percent of Foreign Service personnel take on foreign-born spouses. This, of course, is to be expected when most enter the Service at a fairly young age and spend much of their working lives overseas. But love and statecraft often don't follow in parallel paths and bumps are encountered along the way. Mother State becomes a mutant Junior Prom chaperone when it comes to one's love life and family affairs. You thought you shed parental oversight of your personal affairs once you hit your late teens. But once you take the oath and sign your soul away for that security clearance, be prepared to have your most intimate affairs become the business of Mother State.

Once my relationship with the Dutch peacekeeper became a steady one, the embassy's Regional Security Officer informed me that she needed to be "cleared," i.e., investigated and deemed not a security threat to the United States. "Fill out this Form SF-86 and all these other forms," he told her. She looked at me and asked, "Is this for real?" I said, "Yes, dear. It's only a formality." "I've never dated anyone before whose employer required that I be investigated," she replied, not pleased. The 21-page SF-86 asks such questions as:

"Have you ever knowingly engaged in activities designed to overthrow the U.S. Government by force?"

"Have you ever knowingly engaged in any acts of terrorism?"

The RSO then interviewed her at length. Sheepishly and with unsteady nerves, she confessed to having demonstrated against short-range nuclear missiles in Europe when she was at the University of Leiden. The RSO gave her a pass for this crazy youthful act of anarchistic nihilism. He generously informed us that we could continue to see each other pending a background investigation of her life in the Netherlands.

Now, security investigations have a way of throwing a damper on romance. In the eyes of the foreign ladies, you go from being an eligible bachelor to radioactive waste. Fortunately, I was able to assuage and sweet-talk my foreign lady into going along with what for her was a low-level inquisition. She was "cleared" not long afterward.

Fast forward: Our Engagement. According to the regs. 3 FAM 4191, "an employee intending to marry a foreign national must provide notice 90 days prior to the marriage date." More red tape to complete. The regs further warn, "Failure of an employee to provide the required notification/approval of cohabitation with or marriage to a foreign national may result in the initiation of an appropriate investigation, immediate suspension (which may result in a proposal for revocation) of the employee's security clearance, and/or disciplinary action." Pretty heady stuff. More assuaging and sweet-talking needed.

We put in all the paperwork and made arrangements to wed at a small castle in a fairytale setting in Nijmegen. The entire Dutch extended clan was invited. Everything was on track.

All we needed was the actual green light from Mother State. As time drew down, we continued to wait for that green light. And waited. Finally, I got on the phone and called State. "What gives?" I asked. "It's been months now." I was told to wait some more. Still nothing. My mind started going off in strange directions. *Was she indeed a bomb-throwing anarchist?* I wondered. *Maybe a card carrying member of the Gouda Workers of the World?* Nope. Mother State lost our paperwork. Advance directly to Go and start anew, I was told. "But we have a whole castle lined up. Half of Brabant province has been invited." "Sorry. No wedding without us saying it's okay," Mother State replied with heartfelt empathy. Desperate, I called a buddy who entered the Service with me who worked in that office. Miraculously, he made things happen. We got the green light to marry.

If you work for Wal-Mart or GEICO or JetBlue, you may live with or marry whomever you want whenever you want. But for those who labor in the twilight reaches of national security, Uncle Sam's cold, boney hand keeps a tight grip. Like some medieval lord, his blessing must be gotten to enter a steady relationship or to take the hand of a beloved in matrimony. *Amor vincit omnia.*

Love, Romance and Sex in the U.S. Foreign Service - Part III: Making Babies

After two years of blissful, carefree living as child-free yuppies, we came up with a wild and crazy idea: Let's make a baby!

Living Amongst the Axis of Evil

We had just arrived in Vietnam and our new embassy to which I was assigned as the first American political counselor since 1975. The embassy building was a towering maze of state-of-the-art communist bloc construction and esthetics, yet another monument to the State Department's galactic incompetence. But I digress. Pending the completion of the lovely art deco villa in which we were to be housed, the embassy put us into the Van Phuc diplomatic compound. Van Phuc was one of those gilded ghettoes where communist regimes love to cram foreign officials, the better to keep an eye on them. Our neighbors were Cubans, North Koreans, Russians, Iranians, Libyans, Iraqis and a hodge-podge of other Axis of Evil miscreants. Novosti News Agency, a notorious nest of KGB spies under flimsy journalistic cover, had its offices there as well. Most definitely not a Pleasantville clone. And State's "no-contact" policy with the officials of hostile foreign powers posed an obstacle to chumming it up with the neighbors. Need to borrow a cup of sugar in a pinch? Can't ask the Cuban Garcias – there's an embargo after all. Nor the North Korean military attaché – he might kick your teeth in. Tough it out.

Van Phuc had more concealed surveillance devices than a Mars probe. You just assumed the Vietnamese monitored every movement, phone call, conversation and loose fart. And god knows what our lovely neighbors may have had going on their own. New to such regimes, my Dutch bride needed tips on how to carry on a private conversation with the radio jacked up loud and what to do when funny electronic noises intruded into her phone chats. And on a very sensitive matter, how to go about making babies with the assumption our bugged bedroom was in all likelihood a covert porn set, care of our host government's secret police.

Quack, Quack, Quack

We soldiered on nevertheless. And voila! We conceived a Van Phuc baby! First order of business: see the doctors. The embassy had a contract with an Israeli physician's small clinic. He was an engaging man. Took good care of us. And later was revealed not to have graduated from medical school. Somehow the State Department's due diligence in checking him out wasn't very diligent after all. Then there was the Belgian obstetrician who was one of the revolving door foreign doctors who practiced at Hanoi's SOS Clinic, another embassy contractee. Something about this woman's disco dolly wardrobe and evasive answers regarding her background left me with nagging doubts. Anyway, she did the ultrasound and declared all was A-OK.

State Department as Nurse Ratched

But it wasn't. As the weeks passed, Tosca's belly became very tight, making her unusually uncomfortable. The State Department's regs stipulate that our diplomats may give birth only in the U.S. or other approved countries with advanced and reliable medical establishments. Vietnam is not one of those. We chose South Africa, home of Tosca's parents. Tosca's discomfort grew to the point where our embassy's own doctor submitted a formal request to State's

Medical Unit that she be upgraded to business class for the fourteen-hour airplane travel time from Hanoi to Cape Town, citing her heightened risk for an embolism. Ever alert to protect the lives of its people as well as the unborn, MED denied the request, accusing me of attempting to bilk the system. I shelled out the extra dough to get my pregnant wife a business seat on Singapore Airlines. I later filed a formal complaint to MED's chief regarding the accusation. I received an apology but still no compensation for my wife's airfare.

Not only that, but State would cover only two-thirds of the cost to fly to South Africa. And to top it off, as policy, it provides zero stipend for the husband. Yes, Mother State views its male diplomats as mere sperm donors, unworthy of support to be with their wives when delivering babies. Another out-of-pocket round-trip plane ticket, economy class for myself to join my wife two weeks prior to delivery.

South Africa's medical practitioners and hospitals are among the best. They pioneered the heart transplant. They immediately diagnosed what Dr. Disco Dolly had missed, a very obvious complication. Tosca's belly hurt because she had an overproduction of amniotic fluid. She required urgent relief in the form of draining of some of the fluid. It got worse. To make a long story short, Tosca had to give birth by a scheduled C-section. The baby's esophagus was blocked. Our newborn required major surgery in her second day of life. In the hands of one of South Africa's most renowned surgeons, our baby girl came through after the long operation and ten days sedated in the pediatric ICU.

The ob-gyn physician who had delivered our baby, another one of the country's top-flight specialists and also a great guy, needed to get paid. State wasn't coughing up the money, with no explanation. Doctors there must cover the operating room expenses. It's a huge outlay for them. Our doctor was out of pocket for months. He finally got paid, but informed the embassy that he would no longer treat its personnel.

When our daughter required follow-up surgery two years later, State's Medical Unit accused the surgeon (the same man who had saved her life just after her birth) of overcharging and refused to pay. This surgeon was beside himself and terribly embarrassed. My aggressive interventions got that reversed. Yes, another world-class medical professional who now refuses to treat U.S. diplomats and their family members thanks to Dickensian functionaries who have cold hard steel in place of hearts and shit for brains.

There's a dual irony in this: the State Department merely fronts the money, to be reimbursed by the employee's insurance company later; and one can get top flight medical care in South Africa for a fraction of the cost stateside. My insurance company paid State back promptly and in full, more than glad for such a bargain deal.

End of a Career

Fortunately, our second daughter's birth, also in Cape Town, went quite smoothly. But it was Mother State's heartlessness and unfathomable incompetence that hastened my departure from a career I had loved. No way would I again risk the lives of those dearest to me by being in the employ of Mengele's heirs.

Sin, Sex & Uncle Sam

Of the delights of this world, man cares most for sexual intercourse, yet he has left it out of his heaven. ~ Mark Twain

Back when I was a young diplomat, I took a flight from Bangkok to Taipei to catch an American freighter to Seattle. A Taiwanese businessman on my flight took a liking to me and we exchanged cards. I toured the sites during my weeklong stay in the Taiwan capital. One night, I received a call from the businessman. "Did you receive a visitor this evening?" he asked. I replied that I hadn't. "Didn't a beautiful young woman come to see you in your room?" he persisted. "No," I replied, wondering where this conversation was going. The businessman expressed disappointment and went on to tell me he had hired a high-class "escort" to show me "a good time." He undertook to follow up to ensure the woman returned. I told him I wasn't interested and to cancel whatever transaction he had made with the escort. I then hung up. Why didn't I accept the businessman's "gift"? Several reasons. Prostitution is not my thing, whatever name one chooses to call it. As an official of the USG, I was prohibited from accepting any gift, material or in kind, above a nominal value. The Taiwanese intelligence service was considered a "hostile service" by us, notorious for seeking to suborn U.S. officials by any host of methods, the "honeypot" included. Finally, I've always felt a responsibility to represent myself honorably as an American diplomat abroad. Call me crazy. But that's how I am.

On the heels of the Secret Service prostitution scandal, comes a report out of Brazil of an altercation between members of the U.S. embassy there and a Brazilian prostitute. Romilda Aparecida Ferreira, the ex-prostitute, states she plans to sue for "medical expenses, lost income, and psychological trauma" after an embassy van ran over her in a parking lot leaving her with a broken collarbone, punctured lung and other injuries on Dec. 29, 2011. The embassy personnel comprised three Marine guards and a civilian who took a chauffeured embassy vehicle to a strip club that evening. Ms. Aparecida was one of several prostitutes brought into the van. The Americans reportedly shoved her out of the van before running her over. Ms. Aprecida states she refused a cash payment offer by embassy reps to settle the case. The U.S. State Department confirms the incident took place, but disputes some of the details. Marine guards at our overseas missions, unfortunately, not infrequently land in trouble for misbehavior. Most of them being post-adolescents, it comes with the territory of male youth. Clayton Lonetree, a USMC guard in Moscow who fell into a classic KGB honeypot trap, is the most egregious example.

Meanwhile, Seattle's KIRO television reports that members of the Secret Service advance team paid for sex with prostitutes in El Salvador while preparing for President Barack Obama's trip to the Central American country in March 2011:

"The eyewitness says he joined about a dozen Secret Service agents and a few U.S. military specialists at a strip club in San Salvador a few days before President Obama and his family arrived in El Salvador to meet with its new president, Mauricio Funes.

This source witnessed the majority of the men drink heavily ('wasted,' 'heavily intoxicated') at the strip club. He says most of the Secret Service 'advance-team' members also paid extra for access to the VIP section of the club where they were provided a number of sexual favors in return for their cash. Although our source says he told the agents it was a 'really bad idea' to take the strippers back to their hotel rooms, several agents bragged that they 'did this all the time' and 'not to worry about it.' Our source says at least two agents had escorts check into their rooms. It is unclear whether the escorts who returned to the hotels were some of the strippers from the same club."

These additional sex scandals involving American officials overseas play right into the hands of anti-U.S. Latin American leaders, particularly in Venezuela and Cuba, who throw out facile assertions that Americans historically have viewed the region as a "vast whorehouse." They also leave the average Joe and Jane back home scratching their heads wondering about the caliber of people their tax money is supporting overseas.

So, what gives?

First, it must be kept in mind that when you take the oath to protect and defend the Constitution, you do not also swear to lead the life of a monk. Government is a human institution made up of real human beings, with all the fallibilities and passions inherent in our species. On the other hand, however, those entrusted with representing their country to the world, be they diplomats, military, or law enforcement agents, are expected to comport themselves with dignity and honor.

Unfortunately, this isn't always the case. Again, as a young diplomat at a posting in a communist country, it fell upon my shoulders to negotiate a monetary settlement with a family whose daughter was seriously injured by a drunken embassy communications specialist who drove his car into a group of kids after a night on the town. This married man had repeated scrapes with bargirls as well as traffic cops. When in charge of a consulate in an Asian city, I demanded that our embassy remove a consulate staffer for repeated rabblerousing in local bars and with prostitutes as well as for several DUI traffic incidents. An employee of "another agency," this Oklahoma ex-cowboy married to a devout Baptist spouse just lost it during his first overseas tour of duty.

These are just two of many examples I can cite of bad behavior overseas by some of our officials. I addressed this in more detail in my three-part series, *Love, Romance & Sex in the U.S. Foreign Service*. I concluded, "The U.S. Foreign Service consists of America's best in terms of brains, abilities and relevant knowledge. But its members are all too human just like the rest of us. No, Foreign Service personnel are not a bunch of kinky perverts lusting after the people with whom they work and associate. But funny things do happen in life. And the system is pretty good about policing itself. Messy adulterous affairs overseas often end up with the involved parties being sent back home, with a cloud over their careers. Our diplomats are held to high standards which are taken seriously."

Unfortunately, revelations of carousing by Secret Service agents calls into question that agency's culture as well as its leadership. In a rigorous investigative report in 2002, *Secrets of the Secret Service*, *U.S. News & World Report* revealed a litany of criminal as well as malfeasant behavior on the part of USSS agents ranging from embezzlement to assault to statutory rape going back years. The documented cases cannot be chalked up to "boys will be boys." The central question therefore is whether the Service has truly cleaned up its act, or simply swept problems under the rug. Obfuscatory statements by past directors and the current senior management don't provide a lot of confidence. Those in the service of their nation are human beings. But they are human beings held to a higher standard. The Secret Service motto, "Worthy of Trust and Confidence," needs to be taken seriously by all of its employees. And its leadership, heretofore given a pass by Congress, needs to be held more accountable.

U.S. Secret Service & Scandal

It is imperative, as part of our sworn duties, to always act both personally and professionally in a manner that recognizes the seriousness and consequence of our mission. ~ Mark Sullivan, Director, U.S. Secret Service

I tell him, 'Baby, my cash money!' ~ unnamed Colombian prostitute in a dispute with a Secret Service agent

"Should the shit hit the fan, you grab the President's left arm and I'll grab his right and we shove him with all our might into that doorway over there, got it?" the Secret Service agent instructed me as President Bill Clinton was about to complete inspection of a Vietnamese military honor guard at the ornate French colonial presidential palace in Hanoi on Nov. 16, 2000.

At the time, I was a Foreign Service officer serving as chief of political affairs at our embassy in Vietnam. During an advance team planning meeting, the Secret Service special agent in charge issued me a special access pin giving me virtually unhindered access to the president and First Family, essentially deputizing me as an auxiliary member of the commander-in-chief's protective detail. I was selected because of my command of Vietnamese, knowledge of the city, and, apparently, their confidence in my sense of security. I was not, however, issued a firearm, nor one of those curly-wired earphone devices nor even sunglasses. I was taken on as someone who could make the Secret Service's job go a bit more smoothly. It's an experience I'll proudly relate to my grandchildren one day (if I ever have any).

The salacious story about eleven U.S. Secret Service agents and eleven military personnel engaging prostitutes two days before President Obama's arrival in Cartagena, Colombia for the sixth Summit of the Americas cast profound shame on the United States. Personally, as one who has worked closely with the Secret Service, I found it deeply saddening. My dealings with Secret Service agents during my quarter century of government service always impressed me that these were the cream of the cream, exceptionally dedicated and skilled professionals entrusted with the safety of the president and others whom they protected.

At least six Secret Service agents were forced out. Two were supervisors and three were counter-assault team members. Five others were under investigation, as were eleven members of U.S. military services. Under the Uniform Code of Military Justice, patronizing prostitutes is a crime for military personnel. It is also prohibited by regulation for members of the U.S. Foreign Service. The Secret Service's code of conduct prohibits immoral conduct without being more specific.

Rules on personal conduct, however, are almost beside the point. Two other considerations are more paramount: security and image. By bringing uncleared persons (in this case, Colombian prostitutes) into their hotel rooms, agents not only endangered themselves, but by leaving their IDs, badges, guns and possibly schedules of presidential movements in the open, they also endangered the president. They opened the door as well to possible blackmail. The "honey trap" is one of the oldest espionage lures in the books. Those who work in national security with top secret clearances are trained to be vigilant against hostile players such as foreign intelligence services and terrorist groups who seek to compromise U.S. officials.

As for image, all Americans who are entrusted with serving their country abroad have a special unspoken responsibility to show the United States in the best possible light by dint of their professionalism and personal comportment. Visiting strip clubs and engaging whores two days prior to a visit by the U.S. president, needless to say, does the exact opposite. Furthermore, the supervisor who put up a photo on his Facebook page of himself on a Sarah Palin protective detail with the caption, "I was really checking her out, if you know what I mean?" is at least guilty of terminal stupidity.

"I'm just shocked this happened. We were instructed never to party — even on our own time," said Bill Holland, who worked as a uniformed division officer. This sentiment reflects that of the vast majority of the 3,500 agents and 1,400 uniformed officers of the U.S. Secret Service. The Cartagena incident followed the November 2009 fiasco when several agents allowed two uninvited guests onto White House grounds for a state dinner and photo shot with the president. The so-called "Gate-crasher" incident led to three agents being placed on administrative leave. The Service does not need more of this kind of publicity. Its mission is to carry out its dual duties of VIP protection and investigating financial crimes without fanfare or controversy.

Ronald Kessler, author of the book *In The President's Secret Service* and a critic of the former director, said the incident "is a symptom of the corner cutting and laxness that has been going on under Director Sullivan." The Service is being burdened with more duties without adequate resources to support those added duties. Cutback on overtime pay and lack of concern over agents' personal lives have led to difficulties in staff retention and recruitment. "Most of the time they're so exhausted they don't even have a home life," Kessler said.

Clearly, Congress needs to take a broader look at the Secret Service, beyond this scandal. A thorough review of management, training and resources is glaringly needed with an eye toward reform so that those responsible for protecting our leaders can do their job efficiently and with the knowledge that they have the full support of the American people.

Sex and the CIA: The Abrupt Fall of Gen. David Petraeus

On the sudden resignation of Gen. David Petraeus over an adulterous affair, political pundit David Brooks lamented that we couldn't have a more "French attitude" toward such human peccadilloes. Indeed, the CIA's third and longest serving director, Allen Dulles, was a notorious serial adulterer who reportedly had sex with the Queen of Greece in his office. So, why drum one of America's most brilliant generals out of office in the bat of an eye?

Three reasons:

- the Uniform Code of Military Justice defines adultery as a crime which "brings discredit upon the armed forces (and is) conduct prejudicial to good order and discipline." Furthermore, retired members of the uniformed services who are entitled to retirement pay are also subject to the UCMJ. Therefore, Petraeus's retired status does not exempt him from military justice. There is also the open question concerning "the misuse, if any, of government time and resources to facilitate the commission of the conduct," another violation of the UCMJ.

- moral transgressions among those working in national security potentially make those officials vulnerable to compromise by hostile intelligence services. By keeping secret an adulterous affair, the CIA's top official opened himself up to blackmail.
- as a four-star general and Director of Central Intelligence, Petraeus is expected to hold himself to a high moral example to those who work for him. Tawdry personal behavior is not to be tolerated. Allen Dulles lived in an era when the media generally did not report the sexual escapades of the country's political leaders. That is not the case today.

████████████████████████████████████ attitude toward adulterous affairs, drinking problems and mental health issues ██████████ ███████████ to be quite tolerant. Superiors generally counseled those with behavioral issues as a first resort, using punitive measures only when counseling didn't work. Embassy personnel ████████████████████ serving in hostile nations, however, were yanked out quickly when found to be engaged in adultery since, again, they opened themselves up to potential blackmail. Even dating foreign nationals required disclosure to security officers, as I found out when I began seeing my future wife, who was Dutch.

The FBI reportedly stumbled upon the Petraeus-Paula Broadwell connection in the course of investigating threatening emails sent by Ms. Broadwell to a female associate of Petraeus's via Gmail. It is well known that the Chinese, Russians, North Koreans and others aggressively target U.S. government agencies and personnel via the internet, prying secrets wherever and whenever they can. Employees of the intelligence agencies, the military and the State Department receive regular briefings and admonishments on safeguarding classified information from such digital prying. Petraeus may have made himself vulnerable in his careless use of personal emails.

And there's likely more to this story than what's been revealed so far. The FBI does not routinely investigate cases of threatening emails. This normally is not their job. A federal crime must be in the making. Furthermore, a court warrant must be obtained before they can eavesdrop on an American citizen. Finally, the FBI's investigation apparently was months in the making. There may be a mountain under this mole hill of an adulterous affair.

How such a brilliant public servant as Petraeus could entangle himself in an affair he knew could destroy his career, not to mention his marriage, is anybody's guess. He was famous for his judicious public persona, circumspection and self-discipline. But he is also human, like the rest of us. If an adulterous affair is the only thing behind his abrupt resignation, he certainly has more he can contribute by heading a prominent academic institution, think tank or other non-governmental organization once the dust has settled. David Petraeus's last chapter has not been written.

What's Wrong With America's Generals?

*Liar. Cheat. User. Hustler. Brad Carlton was all of these things.
Then he took advantage of women. Or worst of all,
hid behind their skirts.*
~ Victor Newman (Eric Braeden) on *The Young and the
Restless*: Episode #1.9078" (2009)

- Army Brigadier General Jeffrey Sinclair, formerly deputy commander of the 82nd Airborne Division, has been charged with forcible sodomy, wrongful sexual conduct, inappropriate relationships, fraud, forgery, and possession of alcohol and pornography while on deployment.
- Gen. William "Kip" Ward, who formerly led the U.S. Africa Command, was stripped of a star and forced to retire after accusations of spending thousands of dollars on lavish travel and other financial improprieties.
- Brig. Gen. Roger Duff was dismissed from the military for conduct unbecoming an officer for wearing unauthorized awards or ribbons and making a false official statement.

- In 2005, four-star Gen. Kevin P. Byrnes was forced to retire after engaging in an extramarital affair.
- In 1999, Maj. Gen. David Hale pled guilty to charges related to adultery and was ordered to retire at a reduced rank.

If the U.S. government's national security leadership is increasingly taking on the cast of a soap opera, the headlines certainly bear it out. As with most people, I had a hard time keeping up with what general has been hitting on which married woman, one of whom was being hit up by a shirtless FBI agent, and so on and so forth. The writers of *The Young and the Restless* could not conjure up a more outlandish and tawdry plot. But, as the above cases show, hanky-panky among the country's top military brass is nothing new. It's just that we've had a cluster of them lately. Gen. Douglas MacArthur had brought home his film actress mistress from the Philippines. He subsequently dispatched his aide, Dwight Eisenhower, to pay her $15,000 to go away. She later committed suicide. Eisenhower, himself, is rumored to have had an affair with his chauffeur, Kay Summersby.

What accounts for this Generals Gone Wild behavior among men who spent decades honing self-discipline and rectitude, expected to act as moral examples to those under their command?

While assigned to the Naval War College in the '90s, I befriended a civilian psychologist who counseled Naval personnel. Without naming names, my friend outlined a picture among officers as well as enlistees of widespread substance abuse, depression and domestic violence behind the Navy's veneer of retro-family values. A report by the Defense Department's Family Advocacy Program shows that in 2010, the spousal abuse rate was 11.2 per one-thousand couples, up from 10.1 per thousand in 2009 and 9.4 per thousand in 2008. The rate had been steadily declining from 16.5 per thousand in fiscal year 2001. Furthermore, there were sixteen domestic abuse deaths in 2010. In 81 percent of the cases, the perpetrator was an active-duty soldier. Also, the number of confirmed child maltreatment cases rose from 4.8 incidents per one-thousand children in 2008 and 2009 to 5.7 per thousand in 2010. DoD reports prescription drug abuse doubled among U.S. military personnel from 2002 to 2005 and almost tripled between 2005 and 2008. Alcoholism is also on the rise, particularly among troops returning from combat duty. Also, 20 percent of active and 42 percent of reserve component soldiers are in need of mental health treatment. A sustained and intensified ops tempo resulting from fighting two wars is largely behind these trends.

Gen. Petraeus commanded combat troops in Iraq and Afghanistan for a total of six years, following which he took the reins of CIA director, hardly a low-stress job. He was treated in 2009 for early stage prostate cancer. The man has hardly taken a break in years. One wonders how the incessant stress has affected his judgment. Behind the surface of uber-General is a human being, subject to the same vulnerabilities as many of us.

Perhaps we need to take a closer look at the hyper-moral codes to which our military personnel must strictly adhere.

Our allies tend to be less rigid than we are in this area (though the Canadians sacked their commander in Afghanistan a couple of years ago for having an adulterous affair with a female subordinate.) Flag officers are citizen soldiers. Those stars on their shoulders lead a few to hubristic or reckless behavior. My take, however, is that they are subject to the same weaknesses of the flesh and judgment as businessmen, teachers, doctors, butchers, bakers and candlestick makers. Shakespeare hit the nail on the head: "I am driven on by the flesh, and he must needs go that the devil drives."

ESPIONAGE AS VAUDEVILLE

On Spies, Counterspies, Would-be Spies and Just Plain Losers - Part I

The best quality of a spy is patience.
~ Yakov Peters, Chairman of the Soviet Cheka

I point out in my essay, *Why I'm Censored,* that one signs away a part of one's soul for life when joining the confraternity of national security. I described how I am legally bound to submit to government censors for security review all of my writings prior to publication. Technically speaking, I am required to clear all public speaking materials as well. I must submit to this restriction of my freedom of expression until the day I die. I am not an oracle of secrets. I am just one of countless former officials who are under the same restrictions. It goes with the territory. It makes one wonder, however, why bother when some jerk army private can steal and release to humanity hundreds of thousands of classified documents? But that's above my pay grade.

I served in one capacity or another in four communist countries: Vietnam, Laos, Cuba and Cambodia (before it changed political systems). Moreover, I had traveled throughout China. In each of these countries I was a target of constant surveillance and occasional harassment or recruitment by dint of being an American official. Sometimes it was scary; other times laughable; but usually it was merely annoying. Looking over my shoulder or in the rearview mirror, running surveillance detection runs, mincing my words over the phone, conversing with the radio turned up loud, and increased general reticence became second nature to me and continues with me to this day. There is much I cannot reveal. But that which I can divulge sheds some light on the world of spies, security and secrecy.

Laos in the early 1980s was a satrapy of Vietnam, a communist dictatorship overrun with all manner of East Bloc denizens. Our tiny American embassy there was our sole diplomatic post in Indochina. Our relations with Vientiane were tenuous at best. I was followed, threatened and cajoled by agents of Laos, the Soviet Union, Vietnam, East Germany and Hungary. Yevgeny, a young English-speaking Soviet KGB officer posing as a diplomat trolled the Australian Club, a popular watering hole for Westerners, for loose chatter and potential spy recruits. He attempted repeatedly to ingratiate himself with me in a variety of venues. I rebuffed him every time and warned other Westerners to avoid the smarmy creep. A KGB colleague of his had a different mission. As my network of Lao friends expanded, this bald fire plug of a thug followed me blatantly in his claptrap Lada in an effort to intimidate me. One night, as I left a party, he tailgated me and put his headlights on bright. Accepting the challenge, I took the guy on a nocturnal wild goose chase on dirt roads outside the city in my 200 hp V8 embassy Chevy Malibu. I'd speed, then slam on the brakes to kick up clouds of red dust. I did this repeatedly until he gave up (no doubt coughing his lungs out). Eat dirt and die commie bastard!

The most pathetic recruitment attempt, however, came from the Hungarians. Days after my arrival in Laos, two young Lao girls arrived at my villa and asked to come in. They told me they wanted to show me "a good time." Smelling a rat, I demanded to know who sent them. "Nobody," they replied. "Don't give me that," I shot back. "Now come on, tell me who sent you here." "The Hungarian Embassy," they giggled. "How much did they pay you?" I asked. They told me. It was my fluent Lao and sense of humor that loosened the girls up. Some dumbass Hungarian spook with too much time on his hands and too few brains attempted lure me in what the spy world calls a "honey trap." Loser.

When I moved into my residence in Hanoi with my young family in 1998, Vietnamese residents dropped by to introduce themselves to their new American neighbors. Some bore small gifts of welcome. They clearly were fascinated with Americans and adored our babies. Each morning as I left to walk to the embassy, our neighbors would wave and say good morning. Shortly afterward, it all turned cold. No more visits by our new friends. No more morning greetings. People avoided eye contact and went on their way. One, however, confided to me that the secret police had come into the quarter to warn everyone to stay away from us. I subsequently detected a twenty-four-hour surveillance post set up in the building opposite our villa. They spent the next four years observing us changing diapers and listening to us discussing past episodes of Masterpiece Theatre. Hope our monitors got hardship pay.

By the way, guess who turned up in Hanoi like a bad kopek? My old friend, Yevgeny! Still trolling for "assets" among foreigners seventeen years after I first encountered the son of a bitch. Naturally, I went around to all Western diplomats blowing the whistle on the Big Bad Wolf Yevgeny.

The worst of the lot, however, were Cuban agents of the Ministry of Interior (MININT). On a two-week official trip through the length and breadth of the island, my U.S. Interests Section colleague and I were heavily surveilled and tailed wherever we went. MININT agents are notorious for making the lives of American diplomats as difficult as possible, including stealing clothing articles, downloading our hard drives, smearing dog feces on our door handles and slashing our car tires. I made a point of carrying with me everything I valued in a canvas attaché bag wherever I went, including at the beaches. In Santa Clara, our tires were slashed. My hotel room in Santiago was equipped with listening devices and hidden cameras. The worst thing one can do is to fight back or to otherwise intimidate any nation's secret police. Usually, in fact, both sides reach a modus vivendi. They're doing their job. You're on the up-and-up (usually anyway). Let them follow you. Be civil. Do not provoke. *But*, I couldn't help jotting down verse of Dr. Seuss and Lewis Carroll, putting "CONFIDENTIAL" at the heading and leaving the papers carelessly around my hotel rooms. Now, what does "Twas brillig and the slivy toves did gyre and gimble in the wabe…" mean? Must be some infernal code.

I like to incorporate such experiences in my thrillers. I went through the wringer with the government censors on my novel, *Tribe*, and was compelled to make redactions and changes. But most remained intact. *Permanent Interests* is chock full of insights into the Russian SVR (formerly KGB) and the world of spies. It also gives a glimpse into how my old employer, the State Department, operates. And the State Department redacted sentences and passages in this book.

On Spies, Counterspies, Would-be Spies and Just Plain Losers - Part II: An Open Letter to Anna Chapman

Dear Anya Vasilyevna Kushchyenko Chapman,

We miss you. We miss your Clairoled red hair splashing color across our TV screens during our drab gray recession. We miss your sassy smile and accounts of your escapades clubbing around Manhattan. We miss reading about your Boris & Natasha espionage exploits as the FBI was on to you from the moment you stepped on American soil. We miss your trendy outfits, especially the gray one that makes you look like a toy soldier. We miss revelations on how you wrapped libidinous, social climbing NYC male nobodies around your little Salon 25-manicured finger. If Woody Allen were to make a spy spoof, you would be a natural for the female lead.

But, alas, you can't return to the Big Apple, though your attorney revealed you dearly wanted to. What? Can't get a decent apple martini in Moscow? Poor thing. Not only are you blacklisted here, but the British government revoked the UK citizenship you acquired from your ten-minute marriage to that loud-mouthed English nerd. That scotched your plans to resettle in that country as well.

What's wrong, Anna? Is life so terrible in Mother Russia? Tired already of inaugurating tractor factories and addressing klatsches of pimple-faced Youth Guard drones in Stalinist auditoriums? We all can empathize with you on this. I guess an American version of your particular corner of hell might be volunteering at Lions Club potluck dinners night after night without end. Our hearts go out to you.

But Comrade Putin has pinned medals on you and trotted you out like some legendary race horse. You're a media star in your own country! What more can you want? What's that? The apple martinis at Table 50? Oh yeah. Much better than a stiff Stoli at the workmen's hall of Tractor Factory #58.

"We must transform the future, starting with ourselves," you told that group of Youth Guard drones not long ago. Seriously Anna, I think you need a new complete makeover. Let's start with your spy tradecraft. Sending messages through a dedicated network from your perch at Starbucks in lower Manhattan to your spy handler as he fought New York traffic in a boxy van with Russian dip plates – as the FBI intercepted everything – was a scream. Will you let Woody put that one in his movie? And your writing "99

Fake St." for your home address on the invoice (also intercepted by the FBI) of the cell phone you purchased to make
an urgent call (also intercepted) to your KGB/SVR father
in Moscow to seek guidance concerning the phony passport
you naively accepted from an FBI agent posing as a Russian
spy – well, Woody is rolling on the floor in uncontrollable
laughter over that one.

Next, we simply must stop this femme fatale nonsense.
Let's face it. You have a dental hygienist's face grafted onto
a thirteen-year old's corpus. If you learned one thing in
your aborted stay in NY, it's Madison Avenue-style brand-
ing and packaging. But I, frankly, have seen sexier babes at
church basement pie sales. And, shame on your spy-dad and
mystery-mom for letting you strut your stuff on the cover
of Maxim and Tractor Factory #58's Annual Calendar. Just
more of today's lax parenting, I guess.

BTW, what was it that the SVR tasked you and those ten
other clowns with stealing in NY? Inside dope on Wall
Street? Whoa! Did the FBI ever do Russia a favor here!
Think of it. Transplanting the same criminal financial chicanery that brought down a superpower onto an economy
the size of that of Los Angeles. Tractor Factory #58 would
definitely be shuttered and your cover girl mags and cal-
endars would be used as fuel to warm the hands of the
homeless unemployed. You guys owe us one.

So, let the brown tresses reappear, Anna; wear something
befitting a woman on the cusp of thirty and take a course
in dental hygiene. Russians could use some better dentistry.

P.S. To keep up with the hottest clubs in New York, log on to NBC's *Saturday Night Live*, which you no doubt miss, for the city's "cultural consultant," Stefon – "the hottest club in New York is 'Slash'…"

Another Open Letter to Anna Chapman

Dearest Anya Vasilyevna Kushchyenko Chapman,

To my utter surprise, my open letter to you of March 17 (St. Paddy's Day) 2011 - Open Letter to Anna - has been a h-u-g-e hit, ranking number six in popularity among all of my bloviating expositions. Whether it's the sex that sells (see Anna's racy photos in Maxim) or my caustic humor, you and I are an ideal team. Hence, another Open Letter to Anna in a shameless gambit at furthering my readership and selling more of my books.

So, Anna, here's the deal. I just published my third political thriller, *Tribe*. I'm banking on it joining its predecessors, *CHASM* and *Permanent Interests* on multiple bestseller lists. I'm working on the P.R. and can use some help. Would you be willing to shill for me? In return, I can offer the following: (a) pattern the female lead in my next spy tale on you; (b) promise I'll tone down my sarcastic remarks about you; (c) I'll put in a good word for the reconstituted KGB, i.e., the SVR.

Now, I must confess, I've had plenty of dealings, or should I say run-ins, with the KGB in my adventurous past and none of them was positive (see *On Spies, Counterspies,*

Would-be Spies and Just Plain Losers - Part I). The vast majority of KGB agents I dealt with were sleazebags, Neanderthals, morons and troglodytes. Their official covers were a joke and their tradecraft pretty transparent. Nevertheless, I'm willing to let bygones be bygones and make a deal with you, and only you. Not the comrade in the next photo, whom, one would think, should have more on his mind than body sculpting; like, say, running a country. BTW, twenty years after belatedly annulling the Bolshevik experiment, it's time for Russians to settle down, stop being so sex-crazed and vain. I mean, like, get a life, and stuff!

Believe it or not, Anna, I'm absolutely fascinated with Russian culture. And I even like your food. Your diplomats introduced to me to Siberian-style zakuski and borscht, washed down with arctic-cold vodka. And also the traditional banya. Delightful! So is my favorite composer, Rachmaninoff. My dream is one day to visit Mother Russia and see the Hermitage and many other wonderful landmarks. While I can speak a smidgen of Russian, my training, alas, was in German, followed by several other languages, exotic and mundane.

Now, get this - both *Permanent Interests* and *Tribe* prominently feature Russians. As it happens, the vast majority are heavies. KGB goons and nutso *vory* gangsters. But the SVR agent in *Tribe*, Sergei Nemsky, turns out to be a very sympathetic, human character. His is a touching story about a father and a patriot torn between loyalty to his motherland and saving his daughter. I think *Tribe* is a winner. But I can use some help. Here's where you come in: How about starting out with a review of my book on Amazon? In turn, I'll interview you on my blog and give you free reign to explain yourself and your sordid escapades. Deal? You can reply by posting a comment on my blog or my Facebook page.

Looking forward to hearing from you (or your #1 boss).

Best,
James Bruno

Another Message to Anna Chapman: Never Mind!

Dear Anya Vasilyevna Kushchyenko Chapman,

Guess what? My latest political thriller, *Tribe*, just became a bestseller! Yep. Today, it climbed to no. 98 of the top 100 "Political Fiction" Kindle ebook sales. It's surpassed one of Stephen Coonts's books. *Tribe* is a top seller out of 1,008,648 Amazon ebooks sold; no. 98 out 2,521 Political Fiction ebooks. And my paperback sales haven't been bad either.

And I'm convinced this is only the beginning. Why? Because it's just a terrific read. A veteran Washington journalist described it as having "everything - action, suspense, sex, humor, and, in an American take on John Le Carré's gray world of espionage, a meditation on the bigger issues of trust and betrayal and how to find room for patriotism or integrity in a world of runaway egos and ambition." And, you'll like this: it gives sympathetic treatment to a Russian intelligence officer. More than you ever got (viz., your Mug Shot).

So, Anna, it looks like I won't need your help (see Another Open Letter to Anna Chapman). I thought I'd give a boost to your sagging career as an aging sex siren and failed spy. What's an almost thirty-year old Plain Jane femme fatale to do with her life after all? Surely, giving one insipid speech after another to klatsches of pimple-faced Young Guard drones in Stalinist auditoriums can't compare to Happy Hour at Manhattan's Table-50 with their delicious twenty-dollar apple martinis and coke-fueled yuppies. It's not to say I still couldn't use a genuine Russian spy to help me shill my books. I wonder what Vitaly Yurchenko is doing these days? Last I heard, the former senior KGB officer and re-defector was working as a guard at a Moscow bank. What do you think the future holds for you, Anna? It's not too late to take up dental hygienist as a follow-on career before the crow's feet appear.

You missed your chance, Anna, of re-connecting with your beloved and spurned USA, of jumping back into the limelight. And with me too! A dashing ex-diplomat-turned-novelist who wields his pen like a rapier, onto his third bestseller, no less. Not that I could date you, mind you. I'm preoccupied with making pancakes for the family in the morning and taking my thirteen-year old to see "Rise of the Planet of the Apes."

So, never mind! I retract my previous offer. I'll take your silence as a "No." But then there's always a second chance. My Cuba spy thriller, *Havana Queen*, is now out…

The Anna Chapman Saga Continues:
Not Again! More Russian Spies Arrested

Dear Anya Vasilyevna Kushchyenko Chapman,

You never cease to amaze us! German authorities just arrested more Russian sleeper agents, a married couple who reportedly were in regular contact with you, no less. According to Der Spiegel, "the suspected couple operated more than twenty years under cover in Germany. It is the first such case of 'illegals' since reunification." Details are sketchy at this point, but the couple, whose names are not yet made public, apparently were engaged in industrial espionage. The female suspect reportedly was nabbed just as she was receiving encrypted instructions from Moscow via shortwave radio in her apartment – just like in the movies. Investigators found phony Austrian passports listing bogus Latin American birth places in the suspects' home.

Now here's the clincher: Die Zeit newspaper further reports, "an intelligence service tip from the United States got investigators on the trail of the suspects. The two apparently were in intensive contact with the Russian agent Anna Chapman, busted in 2010 in the United States. Chapman and the couple utilized a shortwave channel regularly."

Anna – the bad news about you just keeps piling up! What gives? Now why would you have been in "intensive contact" with illegals in Germany? I must confess I'm stumped. Were you perhaps exchanging recipes for your favorite apple martini? (An Open Letter to Anna Chapman) Or, seeking photo ops in German men's magazines? Given your silly escapades during your all-too-brief and hilarious stay in Manhattan, I can't believe the substance of your communications was anything serious, like, say, stealing the same Wall Street secrets that brought down the economy of the world's only superpower. We would have gladly forked those over on a Covet ("the coolest lounge in Midtown East") bamboo platter.

Anyway, I will say this about the clowns just nabbed by the Germans: their spy tradecraft was good. Very good. Until they came in contact with you. Your confederates in Germany were able to pull off their ruse for twenty-three years. You lasted only one – and the FBI was onto you from the moment your Roberto Cavalli-clad foot stepped onto U.S. soil. In short, Anna, you burned them through your sloppy tradecraft. Thank you for doing so. It saved the German authorities a lot of time, expense and trouble.

Now, let's talk about your future, Anna. As a woman on the cusp of thirty, you can't expect to continue sashaying around in skimpy outfits for seedy, quasi-pornographic men's magazines indefinitely. You've demonstrated through your bad spying that you can't act, much less continue in the exacting field of espionage. You've not taken up my suggestion to go into dental hygiene. And you never took up my offer to help me sell my political thrillers (see *Another Open Letter to Anna Chapman; Another Open Letter to Anna Chapman: Never Mind!*). Furthermore, your parents have shown themselves as completely incompetent career guides, putting you into spy work – for which you are clearly not qualified – then allowing you to flout your plainness for all the world to see. Tsk, tsk. Modern parents!

Anna. Here's my latest brainstorm to get you out of the cheesy Moscow night scene and those endless, mind-numbing speeches you must deliver to brain-dead Youth Guard drones in Stalinist cafeterias and auditoriums: Become a nun in the Russian Orthodox Church. Yes. I'm serious about this. You've proven you're not good at anything else. Shed the fancy shoes, the soulless clubbing with vapid ne'er-do-wells, the pointless skin shots in those girlie mags. Don a habit, take up the Good Book, repent and search for real meaning in life. The church is looking for good people. Who knows, you could look quite fetching in a formless, black, head-to-toe habit. Make a radically different fashion statement. Anna, Go for It!

Eagerly awaiting your reply,
Jim

Russian Sleeper Agents: Holiday Greetings from the Coneheads

Holiday Greetings to All Russian Sleeper Agents!
~ From the Coneheads

Dear Fellow Aliens:

First, Happy Holidays! We here in Remulak extend warm greetings to all current agents and alumni of the illustrious

Illegals Program, now in its ninth decade. Though we were not with the Russian program, we certainly empathize with you Russians for what you have, or had, to put up with: Big Macs, 24/7 open supermarkets, suburban sprawl, Sarah Palin, the Kardashians and PTA meetings. Simultaneously mind-numbing and fattening. Terrible!

During your years-long training in the SVR's Potemkin American town, you no doubt were indoctrinated in *Saturday Night Live* and us Coneheads as part of American Pop-Culture 101. We lived under deep cover in Paramus, New Jersey for over twenty years after our spaceship crashed on earth. We assumed the lives of average Americans, concealing our true identities as Remulakians, fifty light-years from home. As you can see, we, like you, blended right in, speaking flawless American English and adopting American table etiquette by eating mass quantities. As parental units, Prymaat and I raised our daughter Connie as a typical Jersey girl, steeped in refined Garden State culture, manners and speech.

Vladimir Guryev & Lidiya Guryeva - aka Richard & Cynthia Murphy: You resided and were arrested in Montclair?! Why, we were only twenty-five minutes from each other! Now we know why we never ran into you guys at Fitzgerald's for St. Paddy's Day happy hour. You aren't even Irish! And your thick Russian accents didn't even come close to a Cork brogue. What were your SVR handlers thinking! Then again, who are we to talk? Our "legend" was that we came from "a small town in France." Can you imagine, what with our Ramulakian twang? Handlers = Bumblers. Don't you agree?

Andrey Bezrukov & Yelena Vavilova, aka Donald Heathfield & Tracey Lee Ann Foley: "Don" & "Tracey Lee"? Are you kidding? Sorry. But you guys look like you came off a collective farm out past Irkutsk, not from Mayberry. And who were you supposed to be spying on at Cambridge, Mass? America's political darling, Elizabeth Warren? And, like us, your funny foreign accent just wasn't in sync with your legend. No wonder Harvard stripped you, Don, of your hard-earned MPA. That really sucks.

Mikhail Kutsik & Nataliya Pereverzeva, aka Michael Zottoli & Patricia Mills: Mike, our sources tell us that despite bearing the name of "Zottoli," you didn't know cavatelli from calamari. But they placed you in the state with the highest concentration of Italian-Americans. Brilliant. And Nataliya, your "Canadian" legend didn't hold water. Neighbors pegged you as "Yugoslavian," a nation which, like your cover, no longer exists.

Mikhail Anatolyevich Vasenkov, aka Juan Lazaro and Vicky Peláez: your vocal and rancid anti-Americanism gave you both away, a mistake we didn't make despite America's favoring our galactic enemy, Krypton, over our celestial ally, Kalumer.

Anna Vasilyevna Kushchenko Chapman: I'm afraid your other-worldly hair color was as much a tip-off to the FBI as our Coneheads were to NASA investigators. And, had you adopted a more credible legend, as I did being a cab driver and driving instructor, you might have lasted longer. The thing is, a Manhattanite Russian party girl with no credible income source just didn't cut it. And neither did your tradecraft, which our daughter Connie has patented into a kids parlor game here on Remulak, "Anna: Space Cadet Spy."

Don't feel bad, Russian sleepers. We were nabbed by NASA sleuths who were onto us due to the unusual bend in the earth's gravitational field emanating from our ranch house in Paramus. They turned us over to Air Force security, who whisked us off to Area 51 whence we were exchanged for some astronauts at a neutral base on Mars. As you found out when you returned to Russia, life for us back here on Remulak is difficult. Our daughter was crestfallen not to be able to go to Paramus High's senior prom and we haven't had a Burger King breakfast burrito in years. And Remu-Mart just pales next to Wal-Mart. But we do receive broadcast signals (years later) of *Dancing With the Stars* and *American Idol.* And we've followed your own dramas with avid interest.

But getting back to this Illegals Program. Do you really think "Iron Feliks" Dzerzhinsky was in his right mind when he started up this illegals business right after the Great October Revolution? We don't. Remulak's security service has a dossier on Feliks going way back. And it isn't pretty, let me tell you. How does dope-addicted cross-dresser strike you guys? Okay, okay. Call it Remulakian disinformation. But I can email the file to you any time you'd like to see it. It's been declassified under the Anti-Gravity Open Information Act. We also have a growing file with a lot of dirt on "The Gray Cardinal." But that one's classified.

But it's clear your program is still going strong. The Germans just picked up two Russian illegals who were tasked with spying on an auto parts firm. Auto parts? And this gets us to the central point: History has shown that Mother Russia never lacks enemies, real or imagined. Why, the more paranoid you are, the more enemies you have. It's in the Kremlin DNA. But the cold war ended two decades ago. And America is an open book. All you need to do is to google whatever information you want on the place. And you know what? The Americans don't care! It's what an open society is all about. Even we Remulakians now see this. But, oh! What I'd give for a breakfast burrito right now!

Warm Holiday Wishes,
Beldar, Prymaat & Connie

Happy Birthday Anna Chapman!

счастливый день рождения Анна Васи́льевна Кущенко Ча́пман!

Happy Birthday Anna Vasilyevna Kushchyenko Chapman!

On behalf of all active-duty and retired American diplomats and intelligence officers, I want to extend a hearty congratulations on your attaining the age of thirty! That is, your fourth decade of life. You've achieved more in your life than ninety-nine percent of women your age. According to your LinkedIn page, you've done the following:

VP at KIT Fortis Investments
Head of IPO at Navigator hedge Fund - London
Slave at Barclays Bank - London
Sales at NetJets Europe (private Avaition - {sic}) - London

For some strange reason, your stint in New York as bogus real estate agent/failed spy/party girl are left out, as is all the salacious and notorious publicity that resulted. And there's nothing on your near-nude photo shoots with Maxim and other quasi-pornographic magazines. Well, we all have convenient gaps in our résumés. Some things are best swept under the rug. Certainly, a week in solitary in a NYC jail, forced deportation from the U.S. and being stripped of British citizenship don't cut a great impression with potential business clients.

Whoa! Hold on! What's this "Slave at Barclays Bank"? Just what did they make you do anyway?! A slave? Really? You didn't mean a Slav, I suppose? You already have one typo - "Avaition." But most of us will cut you a break since English is not your mother tongue. Nothing wrong with being a "Slav at Barclays Bank." Like me being a Yank at the U.S. State Department. But you repeat "Slave" further down in your LinkedIn credentials. Was it actually that bad? Please explain to your adoring public just what you mean by that Slave/Slav entry. We'd love to know more.

Getting back to your birthday – thirty is a big deal for a woman. It's when most party girls start thinking seriously about turning in that little Versace number for an apron; about trading the disco dance floor for the altar; about finding a life-mate who will still idolize you when the wrinkles set in; about ditching apple martinis for baby formula; about mom's jeans over the G-string; about the family Christmas card photo over skin shots. The photo on your Facebook page, is a step in the right direction, but only a baby step. You convey glamor, but I guarantee you will convey pathos if you continue such titillating poses as you lurch toward middle age.

Anyway, my purpose for this message is not to mercilessly call the world's attention to your checkered past nor to lecture you on the ravages of aging and the need to act like a grown-up woman in her fourth decade of life. It is to wish you a joyous birthday in your permanent exile from Western Civilization, which we all know you miss dearly. Czar Vladimir is pissing Russians off with his atavistic political heavy-handedness. Your beloved SVR (successor to the KGB) still hasn't recovered from the incredibly entertaining clown show you and your ten cohorts carried on until the FBI guys' sides were splitting so hard they just had to finally round you all up. So, happy B'Day Anna. We look forward to seeing you forsake the limelight and stick to selling widgets and other boring stuff. And do let us all know on your Facebook page when you finally find Mr. Right. Just promise us you won't marry a spy. Then someone in Hollywood would absolutely have to make a sitcom out of your life, or better yet – a reality show!

One final note: I hereby promise to stop annoying you and leave you to pick up the pieces of your sordid life. I promise to stop making fun of your laughable spy "tradecraft" skills, your trading in the Manhattan fast life for turgid speeches before pimple-faced Young Guard drones in Stalinist auditoriums, your parents' flawed childrearing, your dental hygienist's looks and your shameless exhibitionism. Raised a gentleman, I was taught early on to show respect for women of "a certain age."

Finally, my blatantly transparent ploys to exploit your notoriety to sell my books is no longer necessary. As of this writing, my thrillers rank #14 and #25 of all Amazon Kindle books sold (out of over a million titles), and top the Political Fiction, Spy Tales, Action & Adventure and Thrillers lists. Nonetheless, my invitation to you to submit a guest blog post still stands…

And, again, I promise to stop being a provocateur.

Really.

Honest.

Scout's honor.

I swear I'll make a good faith effort.

As *Saturday Night Live's* Tommy Flanagan would say, "Yeah, that's the ticket!"

Anna Chapman Redux: White House Honey Trap?

*[She got] closer and closer to higher and higher ranking leadership…
she got close enough to disturb us. We were becoming very concerned.
They [Chapman and the rest of the spy circle] were getting close
enough to a sitting U.S. cabinet member that we thought we could
no longer allow this to continue.*
~ Frank Figliuzzi, Assistant Director for Counterintelligence, FBI.

Dear Anna:

In my last open letter to you on the occasion of your thirtieth birthday in February (Happy Birthday Anna Chapman!), I promised to lay off your case, give you breathing room to re-tool yourself from a striving strumpet to a levelheaded grown-up woman, even to ponder donning a nun's habit and living according to the Good Book. I felt that I had milked your tarnished salacious reputation in my bald-faced effort to shill my bestselling political thrillers for all I could. And, in contrast to you, I worried about my own reputation: that of a pitiless stalker of a fallen woman (come to think of it, I'm not sure you ever weren't fallen). Anyway, I truly intended to leave you alone forever. Really. Honest. No kidding. Scout's honor. I mean it.

But, like it or not, you keep popping up in the news – and, alas, it's never good news. And this time it's a doozy. The FBI's counterintel chief Frank Figliuzzi, in an interview with the BBC, added, "They were getting close enough to a sitting U.S. cabinet member that we thought we could no longer allow this to continue." So, I have no choice but to weigh in yet again. It's like that scene in Godfather III when an aging Don Corleone says, "Just when I thought I was out, they pull me back in!" But I digress…

According to the original June 2010 indictment against you and your fellow failed spies, it was the frumpy and dumpy Lidiya Guryeva, alias "Cynthia Murphy," who attempted to weasel herself into the circle of an unnamed "prominent-based New York financier" who was friends with a "current cabinet official," also unnamed. One of your Moscow handlers was reported to have remarked, "maybe he can provide [Guryeva] with remarks re U.S. foreign policy, 'roumors' [sic] about White House internal 'kitchen,' invite her to venues."

This is disappointing to your legions of adoring fans, myself included. Frankly, I can't picture Lidiya seducing anybody. Can you? I mean, the SVR paired her with the equally frumpy-dumpy Vladimir ("Richard Murphy") Guryev as if they were mating farm animals. This gets into a whole other sordid aspect of your country's soulless foreign intel agency which I may address in a separate commentary one day.

But all this hoopla about a White House honey trap may be much ado about nothing. An FBI spokesman subsequently clarified, "There is no allegation or suggestion in the complaint that Anna Chapman or anyone else associated with this investigation attempted to seduce a U.S. Cabinet official." Instead, the clutzy "Cynthia Murphy" reportedly was attempting to sidle up to a rich New York plutocrat who co-chaired Hillary Clinton's 2008 presidential campaign. There is no evidence anywhere that you were in this particular picture. Which is understandable considering that you squandered your waking hours getting hammered at Manhattan clubs along with vapid NYC yuppies dancing on the deck of America's financial Titanic. Besides, had you been setting a honey trap for White House officials, you would have blown the entire operation from the get-go, such are your skills in espionage tradecraft.

So, I guess, Anna, you deserve neither the added notoriety of this latest ill-founded report nor, for that matter, more of my gratuitous snarkiness. So, I'll lay off – until next time.

Cuban Spies: Being Followed by Mata Hari's Heiress

My essay, *On Spies, Counterspies, Would-be Spies and Just Plain Losers -Part I*, has been a popular one and I've received steady requests for more. Part II is coming. But the following vignette came to mind during a recent conversation with friends about my time in Cuba.

In "On Spies…," I wrote scathingly about the Cuban intelligence service, Directorio de Inteligencia (DI) – formerly Directorio General de Inteligencia (DGI). Like the old East German Stasi, they permeate everyday life on the island. Snitches, called *chivatos*, could be your mother, brother, lover, anybody. DI agents can be both nuanced and heavy-handed, depending on the circumstances and needs. With

American diplomats, they are both, but more often than not, on the heavy-handed side. I described some of their annoying tactics such as stealing one of our socks, our underwear, or smearing dog feces on our car or residence door handles, or, if they're really pissed at us, slashing the tires of our cars – just to make a point. My car tires were slashed in Santa Clara, home of the Che Guevara Mausoleum & Museum. Fidel declared this altar to the late revolutionary off limit to U.S. officials.

Any time we ventured outside of Havana, we were followed, often blatantly so. I recall in Guantanamo city being tailgated by DGI agents in a claptrap Lada. Fun. In restaurants, it was not unusual to be seated next to a "couple" whose ears and eyes clearly were bent in our direction rather than toward each other. You should never provoke secret police monitors, even when they slash your tires, lest you become the target of steady retribution. Usually, you can establish a modus vivendi with official followers. You go about your business. They watch you. Everybody keeps a safe distance.

But it was in Cuba's second largest city of Santiago that I had what I can describe as a pleasant encounter with a watcher. Perhaps because it was a Sunday and DGI agents preferred to be home watching baseball with the family, the Cuban spooks assigned a novice to follow my colleague and me around the city as we took in some sightseeing prior to catching our flight back to Havana. This monitor was a young, pretty Afro-Cuban girl sporting a fluffy blue dress and ribbon in her hair. Perhaps she was the daughter of a DGI official who was home watching the game. Wherever we went on foot, there was *la bonita* several steps behind, not having a clue how to conceal herself. We paused to take in a tourist site, so would she. She was our shadow. In a park, I walked in a pointless circle, and she followed suit. We'd sit down to rest, so would she. It was a game of Simon Says. We made our way to the Spanish colonial fort of el Morro. *La bonita* was right behind us. We paused to observe the beautiful vista over blue Santiago Harbor. So did *la bonita*. I turned and winked at her with a smile. She smiled back and then turned her head away shyly. We toured the fortress. With our little companion close behind, we studied the cannon emplacements, the ramparts, even the dungeons. Upon leaving the fort, I bought a single bloom from a flower vendor, marched over to *la bonita* and gallantly presented it to her. Nonplussed, she took the flower with a blushy smile and we parted ways.

If only the Directorio de Inteligencia had more Mata Haris like *la bonita*, we might have had normalized relations years ago.

The Shadow War with Iran: Role of Intelligence

There is no place where espionage is not possible.
~ SunTzu, *Art of War*, ch.13

- More than a dozen American intelligence assets in Lebanon and Iran were seized recently by Iranian and Hezbollah counterintelligence authorities; sources report the number of U.S. agents caught inside Iran may number in the dozens. Summary execution is the usual punishment.

- On Nov. 29, 2010, Iranian nuclear physicist Majid Shahriari was fatally bombed by a man on a motorcycle while waiting in Tehran rush hour traffic. His family members were unharmed. A clean hit.

- Minutes later, another nuclear physicist and Revolutionary Guard member, Fereydoun Abbasi Davani, barely escaped an identical attack across town. He had been identified in a United Nations sanctions resolution as "involved in nuclear or ballistic missile activities."

- Later that day, Iranian President Mahmoud Ahmadinejad announced that high-speed centrifuges used to enrich uranium had been damaged by a cyberattack. Experts estimate that up to 1000, or ten percent, of the centrifuges at the Natanz nuclear facility had been destroyed by the Stuxnet worm, a very sophisticated virus whose creation is universally attributed to a nation state.

- On Oct. 11, 2011, Washington charged the Iranian government with a plot to murder the Saudi ambassador to the U.S. with explosives.

Discerning covert actions by national intelligence agencies is like a fisherman closely observing the surface of a body of water to ascertain what is going on underneath. Occasionally, something breaks above the surface – in the case of a fisherman, trout; in the case of covert measures, violent or disruptive actions. A shadow war being waged between the West and Iran is increasingly becoming bareknuckled as a showdown looms over Tehran's evident quest to develop nuclear weapons. While the details of the highly classified covert campaign against Iran are lacking, the broad parameters of the West's efforts can be made out:

- The key actors are Washington and Tel Aviv, with CIA and Mossad in the lead. Secondary actors are Berlin (BND), UK (MI-6) and Paris (DGSE).
- All four are engaged in aggressive all-source intelligence-gathering against Iran. But the more muscular covert action side of the equation falls onto Mossad's and CIA's/DoD's shoulders. Stuxnet was likely the product of a joint Israel-U.S. covert program, while the assassinations logically fall into Mossad's domain, Israel being less encumbered by laws against such actions.
- The European services have proven adept at recruiting Iranian sources to obtain intelligence on Tehran's nuclear program.
- There is a structured intel-sharing arrangement among the Western partners.

The Daily Telegraph reports that Israel is "using hitmen, sabotage, front companies and double agents to disrupt the (Iranian) regime's illicit weapons project" and that Mossad is behind the nuclear scientist assassination hits and Stuxnet cyber-attack.

On the Iranian side, the plot against the Saudi ambassador clearly shows Tehran isn't taking the active measures directed against it lying down. Iranian intelligence has demonstrated no hesitation over the years to spill blood in the form of targeted assassinations and sponsored terrorist acts. The Republican Guard's Quds Force has shown itself to be the spearhead in these active measures.

But this cold war between Iran and the West is heating up. An American academic has called it "the Cuban missile crisis in slow motion." And this escalation poses very serious policy challenges for the West. The latter's strategy is three-pronged:

- Diplomatic
  - including increased sanctions
- Intelligence
  - intel gathering
  - covert measures
- Military
  - advanced contingency planning
  - last resort

The diplomatic effort has been well coordinated with increasing political and economic pressures exerted on Tehran. But it has not deterred the Iranians from their goal of joining the nuclear club.

The intelligence effort has also been well coordinated. It, however, has merely delayed Tehran from its goal. On the U.S. side, Presidential Findings guiding the American intelligence efforts have been bipartisan and have spanned at least three administrations. While interagency coordination has been fairly effective, the 2007 National Intelligence

Estimate concluding the Iranians halted their nuclear weapons program in 2003 has been disputed by our European allies and others at home.

We were fast approaching an inflection point: to exercise the military option, or not. This is where we have seen a divergence of views emerging. The Netanyahu government has been rattling its sabre, showing growing signs that Israel might ultimately have no choice but to launch military strikes against Iranian nuclear targets. Washington, on the other hand, has been tossing out a containment option whereby Iran's inevitable acquisition of a nuclear weapons capability would be accepted as a fait accompli, but its anticipated muscle-flexing in the region would be contained much as the Soviet Union's ambitions were held in check by a united West.

The trouble with a military option is that aerial and missile strikes against Iran's nuclear facilities would knock out only part of its nuclear program, the rest having been assiduously dispersed, disguised and buried deep underground. Tehran has no intention of allowing itself to be vulnerable to an Israeli strike as was carried out against Iraq's nuclear reactor in 1981. Washington and its European and Middle East partners, however, justifiably fear potential political repercussions that could lead to further regional destabilization.

Which gets us to the last possible scenario: regime change. The 2009-2010 mass demonstrations by Iranians in response to rigged elections adds to mounting indicators of widespread dissatisfaction with the mullah-controlled regime. The U.S. and its allies have sought to exploit these fissures in the hope that growing public domestic opposition will eventually lead to regime change:

- In 2006, the U.S. Congress passed the Iran Freedom and Support Act which directed $10 million towards groups opposed to the Iranian Government.
- In 2007, President George W. Bush reportedly authorized a $400 million CIA covert operation to destabilize Iran. He reportedly signed a "nonlethal Presidential Finding" directing the CIA to coordinate a campaign of propaganda and disinformation and of undermining Iran's currency and international financial transactions.
- In 2008, journalist Seymour Hersh reported that "Congress agreed to a request from President Bush to fund a major escalation of covert operations against Iran" designed to "destabilize the country's religious leadership."

So far, the Iranian regime remains intact and Ahmadinejad proved himself a wily and formidable opponent. The central question for Washington and its allies has been whether a policy can be forged that would contain Iran without igniting a hot war. And the role of the allies' intelligence services has centered on how effective they can be in spearheading a shadow war that, so far, has managed only to delay Iranian nuclear ambitions. The recent diplomatic breakthrough with Iran's new leadership offers a new, promising route to defuse the situation. Hats off to the diplomats.

WIKILEAKS FIASCO: YES, WE REALLY DO NEED TO KEEP SECRETS

Why Wikileaks and Its Founder Must Be Hounded to the Ends of the Universe and Utterly Destroyed

This is why Wikileaks is destructive to the point of threatening people's lives. When I was serving in a communist country, the idiot who was our deputy chief of mission sent as an attachment in a regular email to a friend an official report of his conversation with a senior official who was critical of his own regime. We knew the host government monitored our commercial emails and were being constantly reminded by our security office to exercise caution in what we put into such emails. But our fool of a DCM ignored this warning. Almost immediately, the host government let on that they had intercepted the incriminating email and proceeded to put heat on the concerned senior official. He feared imminent arrest and imprisonment. Instead, his name was mud in his own government and the man was sidelined and held under indefinite suspicion. But he came within a millimeter's breadth of being thrown into prison due to a "leak."

Here's another example. When I worked on a top secret White House program involving the safety of the president and his senior staff, someone leaked parts of the program to *The Washington Post*, which dutifully published it. Few, if any, outside of government knew the turmoil this threw us into. An inexplicable "leak" by some irresponsible self-serving dolt had the potential of endangering the president of the United States. We worked in overdrive to re-adjust elements of the program.

Diplomacy has as much need to be conducted totally in the open as does your business, law office, doctor's practice or your own personal affairs. Diplomacy requires confidentiality and trust in order to be effective. The media pundits who argue in favor of all official government communications being held in the open "in the light of day" are either

terminally ignorant, galactically stupid or merely disingenu-
ous. Having known and worked professionally with many
of them, I prefer to believe it's the latter attribute at play.
They're simply too smart to believe what they say in public.

Julian Assange is not a journalist nor a whistleblower. He is
a hacker and self-described anarchist whose mission in life is
to bring down government as an institution, and particularly
the U.S government, which he detests. Wikileaks' unloading
of over a million classified military documents and now a
quarter of a million diplomatic cables is nothing less than
a mega-document dump – indiscriminate and malicious in
intent. Not a leak, but a flood.

It's common sense. If governments can't exchange views
with each other confidentially, or diplomats can't report
frankly, we might as well close down our foreign policy
establishment, which is exactly what a fringe actor like Assange would like to see happen.

The media find reading and publishing these messages titillating, much like reading someone's secret love letters. The
voracious media maw craves this kind of information. But
the effect is incredibly damaging, to U.S. foreign policy and
probably to some people's lives. There is an established and
responsible way for public access to official secrets and that
is through the Freedom of Information Act. I would like
to see more responsible comportment and less disingenu-
ousness among our mainstream media. After all, it's their
country too.

Wikileaks Fallout: Diplomats Aren't Spies – Putting a Diplomat's Work in Perspective

The mega data dump of State Department cables that Wikileaks has unloaded into the cybersphere constitutes a great voyeuristic view into the rarefied work of diplomats. While many observers justifiably heap kudos on our Foreign Service officers for their fine reporting and analysis, most readers are viewing the cables both out of context and with no foundation for comprehending how diplomats go about their business.

Let's take one of the most inflammatory messages: REPORTING AND COLLECTION NEEDS: THE UNITED NATIONS. This cable has drawn sharp criticism from the UN community, who see it as an instruction for U.S. diplomats to spy on UN personnel. This is not the case. Every year, the intelligence community puts together a wish list of information they would like to obtain for a host of reasons. It's their own data dump shopping list. They throw the kitchen sink, and more, into these annual bureaucratic exercises. It's a classic case of work by committee.

Our Foreign Service personnel in the field review the list to get an idea of what Washington wants to know. Generally, Foreign Service officers (FSOs) focus on the major regional and security policy issues, e.g., "Afghanistan," "Iraq," "Arms Control," "Terrorism," etc. to know their reporting priorities. Such requests as obtaining "biometric" information is not normally something an FSO will go after. It's not his or her job as an overt official. The key thing here is the cable's statement: "coordinating with other Country Team members to encourage relevant reporting through their own or State Department channels." I, for one, never sought out biometric or other such intrusive information. Nor can I recall any fellow FSOs who did so. We all knew that that was left to the spies, which we were not. I would have refused an order from a superior to go out and intrusively spy on foreign officials. But I never got such orders either.

The general public needs to understand three essential elements about a diplomat's mission: 1) to keep Washington and other American embassies informed about their country or issue(s); 2)to meet and talk with a wide range of people in order to know what's going on, but also to promote U.S. interests, be they political, commercial, humanitarian, what have you; and 3) this must all be done in confidentiality and trust.

I found myself as a twenty-eight-year old junior diplomat at a small embassy serving as Chargé d'Affaires in place of the ambassador, who left for consultations in Washington. As soon as he departed, border clashes broke out between our host country and its larger neighbor. The host country foreign ministry called me in to ask that we help try to resolve the tensions. What made it interesting was that host country was normally hostile to us. This required delicate diplomacy, starting with reporting the approach to Washington and seeking instructions. My reporting included a candid assessment of the host government's interests and intentions. Had this reporting been blown wide open for the whole world to see, our delicate efforts to help defuse what threatened to become outright war would have met with utter failure. The result might have been escalating conflict with resultant regional instability and loss of lives on both sides. But, our good offices did help defuse the conflict and won us some welcome trust within what was normally an unfriendly host government.

As, again, Chargé d'Affaires years later in Cambodia during the UN-sponsored peace negotiations and national reconciliation efforts in the early '90s, a violent coup d'etat was launched by disgruntled military units led by an ambitious member of the royal family. We discovered quickly that a U.S. ally was double dealing and fanning the coup. It was through our quiet but assertive diplomacy with the UN and other countries that we managed to defuse the crisis and put the wayward ally back in their place. Had our reporting and the State Department's instructions been "open to the light of day," all of this discreet and sensitive diplomacy would have gotten nowhere. The violence would have grown and the peace negotiations might have gone down the tubes.

I was privileged to have been among a handful of officials to have read the transcripts of President George H.W. Bush's conversations with Gorbachev, Kohl, Mitterrand and Thatcher very soon after he consulted them on fast-moving German unification as East Germany was folding. The conversations were detailed and frank. What might have been the course of events had Wikileaks been around to publish the transcripts for the world to see?

Diplomats must be pragmatists who are constantly seeking constructive approaches to resolve thorny issues. To do this, they must earn the trust of the people they deal with. One does not earn trust either by carrying out espionage or by divulging to everyone under the sun the contents of his or her discussions or analyses. A reading of the Wikileaks cables underscores this. The FSOs are shown to be both discreet and pragmatically constructive. They are also damn good writers!

Wikileaks & Me

While doing online research on an unrelated subject the other day, I stumbled upon a trove of State Department cables released by Wikileaks in 2010. Dozens of these cables, most classified, had my name on them either as classifier or as chargé d'affaires in keeping with Department reporting protocols. They provided our embassy's best analysis of our host country and its leadership, often citing sensitive sources.

My heart sank when I saw these documents. I was aware that some of my reporting as a Foreign Service officer was among the documents passed by Pvt. Bradley Manning to Wikileaks, but I had no idea so much of it was part of the quarter-of-a-million leaked State Department cables. Frankly, I didn't want to know. Now I know. The Wikileaks fiasco has gotten very personal for me, more than a decade since my having left government service. I read with dread the excellent candid analyses our embassy officers wrote on foreign leaders, their policy directions, along with policy recommendations for Washington decisionmakers. I say with dread because Manning and his Wikileaks accomplices gave away the farm. By exposing such information, foreign leaders can stay two steps ahead of us in formulating their own policy directions vis-a-vis the United States. The dread further extends to those contacts who assumed we could keep secrets when confiding to us. How many will talk to us now? In my earlier posts on Wikileaks, I likened diplomacy to a poker game. If your opponents know all of your cards, assume the game is over. Wikileaks and its fellow travelers either don't get this, or they are driven by pure malice toward the United States. My take is that they indeed do get it and it's malice that drives them. Their so-called commitment to "openness" and "transparency" is simply cover for their misguided anarchistic beliefs.

Bradley Manning was sentenced by a military judge to thirty-five years imprisonment, of which he is required to serve about a third. Assuming he serves at least half of the sentence, it is a high price to pay for a young man for having acted so irresponsibly. Does the punishment fit the crime? Personally speaking, if he doesn't do the full sentence, no. Thirty-five years is a small price to pay for inflicting serious injury to this country's national security and endangering those who take us into their trust.

You'll have plenty of downtime to ponder your action, Manning. You'll have all the time in the world to contemplate how you pissed away your youth. Your vocal supporters will constantly agitate for your parole. But they, too, will be wasting their time, which is about the only satisfaction that I get out of this whole sorry affair.

Wikileaks Fallout: Observations on a Banana Republic

According to Executive Order 13526 signed by the President on December 29, 2009:

"'Secret' shall be applied to information, the unauthorized disclosure of which reasonably could be expected to cause serious damage to the national security."

"'Confidential' shall be applied to information, the unauthorized disclosure of which reasonably could be expected to cause damage to the national security."

The first day I reported to work as Afghanistan desk officer in the State Department, I found a pink slip on my desk citing me for a security violation. The foul-tempered misanthropic woman who had preceded me in that job had left me a desk stuffed with her junk, including a Canadian cable marked CONFIDENTIAL that she had carelessly left behind. The evening before my first day on the job, Marines had gone on one of their periodic random searches of offices to catch things like this. I ended up taking the rap. No excuses. I was left holding the bag by virtue of desk ownership. That violation stayed on my record for three years. Had I gotten two more such violations, they would have yanked my security clearances and I'd be assigned to the mailroom. Three strikes and you're out. Period.

The government expends tremendous resources on protecting classified materials. What most people don't realize is that the primary mission of the thousand U.S. Marines deployed at 148 diplomatic missions worldwide is to safeguard classified information. The safety of the personnel who generate and consume that information comes third (after protection of the facilities that contain the secrets).

Security is a very, very serious thing in the national security agencies. Classified information is locked in safes inside locked rooms inside locked buildings with guards. In many embassies, classified work, such as drafting cables, must be done in so-called secure conferencing facilities, known to laymen as "bubbles." Working in these overly air conditioned metal cocoons is akin to sitting in a cold crypt equipped with special security enhanced PC's.

We also spend enormous resources on diplomatic couriers, men and women whose job it is to carry and accompany classified materials to, from and between diplomatic posts.

There are a lot of misperceptions and outright false claims in the media now about government secrets in the wake of the Wikileaks fiasco. Blanket assertions are made that "the government classifies too much." Oh, really? How would these pundits know that? It's a facile and false claim based on bias and ignorance.

When I entered government as a lowly analyst at the Pentagon in the '70's, indeed almost everything was stamped at least CONFIDENTIAL. The result was the need for too much secure storage space for all this paper (digital storage hadn't come to the fore yet). With so many safes containing so many documents, the USG needed more rooms. More rooms meant more buildings. Not only that, but more man hours were required to cull and maintain the files. It was crazy as well as needlessly expensive. The Carter administration reformed the system, requiring us public servants to classify many fewer documents and to rely on an unclassified restrictive label for any unclassified materials that nonetheless did not warrant unlimited distribution. Further reforms were enacted under President Clinton.

Statistics thrown out about the enormous growth in the absolute number of classified documents are misleading. This growth can be tied to the growth in the federal national security bureaucracy post-9/11 rather than classification-mad functionaries on security steroids wildly stamping everything SECRET.

There are standard procedures for declassifying documents. One is the declassification schedule requiring that all classified documents have an expiration date attached to them. A close examination of the Wikileaks documents reveals these, e.g., "DECL: 09/01/20." The other procedure entails the Freedom of Information Act whereby any citizen may request past classified documents on a given subject. These historical documents are reviewed by legions of federal retirees sitting in the far recesses of the bureaucracies. Sources and methods may be redacted, but usually, the documents are eventually released in some coherent form. A great repository of declassified documents is George Washington University's The National Security Archive (*http://www.gwu.edu/~nsarchiv/*).

Private Bradley Manning, sitting at a U.S. Army base in Iraq, managed to download a quarter of a million diplomatic messages onto a Lady Gaga CD and walk out the door with it. This single act of an unbalanced narcissist with self-esteem issues has blown a tremendous hole in the national security of the United States. The outcome won't be fatal, but the United States certainly will suffer in terms of trust and efficacy in carrying out its foreign policy. And do not rule out people's lives being on the line, including indirectly – for example, from the exposure of the SECRET "Critical Infrastructure List," a windfall for al-Qaida.

But the U.S. government deserves as much, if not more, opprobrium for its unbelievably lax digital security. One would expect this kind of flub-up from a banana republic, not the world's sole superpower. Yes, the need for more information-sharing was underscored in the wake of 9/11. And this need not be sacrificed. What's direly needed is a totally revamped system to prevent acts like Pvt. Manning's. Technologically, this is not in the same league as putting a man on the moon. It's doable now.

The alternative is going back to a system of lots of papers stuffed into too many safes, a grossly inefficient means which puts too many new desk officers at risk for taking some other schmuck's rap.

Wikileaks Fallout: People in Danger

For those who regard Julian Assange's anarchist's spree of dumping a quarter of a million sensitive U.S. diplomatic cables into the cybersphere as an innocent and justifiable escapade, read the following excerpts from the *New York Times* January 7, 2011 edition:

U.S. Sends Warning to People Named in Cable Leaks

The State Department is warning hundreds of human rights activists, foreign government officials and businesspeople identified in leaked diplomatic cables of potential threats to their safety and has moved a handful of them to safer locations, administration officials said Thursday.

With cables continuing to trickle out, they said, protecting those identified will be a complex, delicate and long-term undertaking.

The most visible casualty so far could be Gene A. Cretz, the ambassador to Libya, who was recalled from his post last month after his name appeared on a cable describing peculiar personal habits of the Libyan leader, Col. Muammar el-Qaddafi. While no decision has been made on Mr. Cretz's future, officials said he was unlikely to return to Tripoli. In addition, one midlevel diplomat has been moved from his post in an undisclosed country.

There is anecdotal evidence that the disclosure of the cables has chilled daily contacts between human rights activists and diplomats. An American diplomat in Central Asia said recently that one Iranian contact, who met him on periodic trips outside Iran, told him he would no longer speak to him. Sarah Holewinski, executive director of the Campaign for Innocent Victims in Conflict, said people in Afghanistan and Pakistan had become more reluctant to speak to human rights investigators for fear that what they said might be made public.

(T)he Taliban had said it would study the Wikileaks documents to punish collaborators with the Americans.

"There are definitely people named in the cables who would be very much endangered," said Tom Malinowski, Washington director for Human Rights Watch.

Government officials are also worried that foreign intelligence services may be trying to acquire the cable collection, a development that would heighten concerns about the safety of those named in the documents.

Only a fraction of the cables has been released so far. The potential for bodily harm coming to human rights activists and other sources is very real. And as for those "foreign intelligence services," you can bet your bottom dollar that they already have the full stash and are combing through them very meticulously. The information they glean will help them neutralize U.S. foreign policy interests for years to come.

Wikileaks: Julian Assange as Dr. Frankenstein

Satan has his companions, fellow-devils, to admire and encourage him; but I am solitary and detested. ~ Mary Shelley. *Frankenstein*

The government of Ecuador expelled U.S. ambassador Heather Hodges. "We have asked that she leave the country as soon as possible," said the Foreign Minister. Reason? The leftist leadership of that country objected to classified cables recently released by Wikileaks which describe in detail how "corruption among Ecuadorean National Police officers is widespread and well-known" and that "this situation is more pronounced at higher levels of power." In other words, the embassy reported a true fact about Ecuador.

U.S. ambassador to Mexico Carlos Pascual felt compelled to resign in face of incessant denunciation by that country's thin-skinned president. Reason? Wikileaks released classified cables in which the American embassy reported, "Official corruption is widespread, leading to a compartmentalized siege mentality among 'clean' law enforcement leaders and their lieutenants." "Prosecution rates for organized crime-related offenses are dismal; two percent of those detained are brought" to trial. In other words, the embassy reported an uncomfortable and universally known truth about Mexican law enforcement officials.

The U.S. ambassador to Libya, Gene Cretz, was recalled to Washington after Wikileaks posted his candid assessment of Moammar Gadhafi's oddball behavior, including his employment of a contingent of female Amazon bodyguards. This, of course, occurred before Libya blew up and at a time when we were trying improve relations with that country.

In Kenya, Wikileaks-released cables put Ambassador Michael Ranneberger in the hot seat with that nation's leadership, particularly over a description of Kenya as a "swamp of flourishing corruption." One member of parliament submitted a motion to censure Ranneberger and have the U.S. government recall him.

I've said it before in. If Assange weren't throwing purloined U.S. government secrets to the four winds, somebody else would be. The ultimate blame goes to the USG itself for its loose controls over dissemination of sensitive material, enabling one lowly and screwed up Army private to download hundreds of thousands of state secrets onto a cd and walk out the door with them. What I question is the intent of Assange and his supporters.

His monied supporters include British film-maker Ken Loach, the socialite Jemima Khan, the journalist and filmmaker John Pilger; Patricia David, a professor, and well known lawyer Geoffrey Sheen. They help Assange financially. Wikileaks' workabees are a mélange of misfits and iconoclasts who appear to be riven with dissension. In any case, one hears the terms "freedom of information," "transparency" and "human rights," amongst others from these supporters as reasons to defend and promote Wikileaks.

Taking the examples cited above, one has to ask how revelation to the world of confidential and truthful embassy reporting on corruption in Ecuador, Kenya and Mexico, leading to the withdrawal of two U.S. ambassadors and marginalization of another, has anything to do with human rights or the legitimate right to information. Will Loach, Pilger, Khan, David and Sheen please open their business files and publish every correspondence, every private financial document, every personal note, letter and email to the world? To put their morals where their mouths are, I call on them to do this. Why shouldn't every citizen of the world not know about lawyer Sheen's clients' secrets? How about

Prof. David's personnel evaluations? And socialite Khan's documented personal views on others in her circles? Pilger absolutely must post on the internet for all to see his journalistic sources and what they've told him in confidence. What deals is filmmaker Loach negotiating behind closed doors and how much is he willing to pay one actor over another? Come out with it! The world deserves to know. Place a webcam over your shoulders, put all of your correspondence on Google docs. Let's not be hypocrites, after all.

My take is that Assange's supporters mainly comprise the naive, the stupid and those who are driven by malice. What's being revealed is not today's equivalent of the Molotov-Ribbentrop pact, but plain, hard truths about other governments conveyed to U.S. leaders by their official envoys. Like it or not, truth often requires discretion and, yes, secrecy. Without it, we might as well shut down our national security establishment and return to a nomad hunter-gatherer society.

Assange has created an out-of-control monster called Wikileaks whose victims keep piling up. His supporters are fawning Igors who leer and cheer him on. Mary Shelley would write a book about them at the drop of a quill pen.

Wikileaks: The Strange Case of Julian Assange & Ecuador

After Britain's highest court ruled against Wikileaks founder Julian Assange on his extradition case to Sweden for having allegedly committed sexual crimes there, the Australian firebrand has hightailed it to Ecuador's London embassy seeking "political asylum." Just when we thought we've seen all the crazy gambits this fellow is capable of, he tops it with another. And this one is a doozy. I wrote about the complications of a person's seeking diplomatic asylum in a foreign embassy recently in connection with Chinese citizens crashing U.S. diplomatic missions in the PRC. (*Diplomatic Asylum: Why an Embassy Isn't Embassy Suites*). He chose Ecuador for two reasons: a) Ecuador's current leader, Correa, is an anti-American leftist who has known Assange previously; and b) Correa made the U.S. ambassador in Quito persona non grata last year following Wikileaks' release of classified embassy cables reporting on corruption in Ecuador. Correa's ambassador to the UK has two choices: a) "invite" Assange to depart the premises, whereupon UK authorities will arrest him; or b) prepare for hosting a surprise house guest in her tiny embassy indefinitely.

The legal picture does not look good for Assange. The Guardian newspaper (June 20, 2012) lays out it all out pretty clearly:

Q: If Julian Assange remains inside the Ecuadorean embassy, how long can the standoff last?

A: The Foreign Office have confirmed that while he is on diplomatic territory, he is "beyond the reach of the police". Officers may only enter the building in Knightsbridge if invited inside by embassy officials.

Q: Is there any way the Ecuadoreans can spirit him out of Britain and ensure he reaches the safety of Quito, their capital?

A: If Assange steps out of the embassy, he is liable to be arrested. Were he to be given a diplomatic passport, that would not alter the situation: immunity from arrest is only conferred on diplomats accredited to the Court of St James's by the Foreign Office.

Any attempt by the Ecuadoreans to have him accredited would be rebuffed by UK authorities. Were Assange to accept an Ecuadorean diplomatic passport, some suggest, he would become an Ecuadorean national – and therefore be unable to seek asylum in what would now be his own country's embassy. Diplomacy is a cunning profession – dangerously double-edged.

Q: Has there been a similar act of diplomatic defiance in UK history?

A: The Foreign Office could not recall a recent parallel. Even cases abroad are relatively rare. In 1956, the US granted the Catholic Cardinal József Mindszenty refuge in their Budapest embassy; he stayed for 15 years.

Seven Pentecostalists who burst into the US embassy in Moscow in 1978 seeking asylum remained in its basement until 1983. Six Cubans crashed a bus through the Peruvian embassy gates in Havana in 1980; Peru refused to hand them over whereupon Castro removed security guards from the embassy perimeter, allowing more than 10,000 Cubans to flood into the embassy grounds.

Two of the most recent embassy asylum cases involved refugees from China. In February this year, a police chief entered the US compound but was persuaded to leave after 24 hours. The Chinese dissident Chen Guangcheng escaped house arrest in his native village and sought sanctuary in the embassy in Beijing. He later flew to the US.

Q: Can the Swedish authorities bring any legal challenge against the Ecuadorean government, forcing them to hand over Assange?

A: It is difficult to see how that might happen. Swedish prosecutors have indicated that they do not wish to become further involved until Assange is flown to Stockholm. The Crown Prosecution Service says that it acts on behalf of the Swedish authorities.

Q: Why is Sweden seeking to extradite Assange to Stockholm when he has not been charged with any offences?

A: In Sweden, it is normal practice for prosecutors to question suspects face-to-face before they are charged. European arrest warrants issued by Sweden against other suspects have run into similar objections – that the suspect being sought has not been charged – in other European countries.

Q: Are the Americans also seeking Assange in connection with his Wikileaks revelations?

A: It is not known whether there is a sealed indictment against him in the United States. A grand jury has been empanelled in Virginia to consider his case. Any US extradition request, it is assumed, would have to wait until Swedish justice had dealt with Assange.

Let's see who's dumber – Assange in trying to be a latter-day Cardinal Mindszenty, or the Ecuadoreans in dissing the UK legal system. In the meantime, Madame Ambassador, stock up on Vegemite.

Assange Case: Can the British Storm Ecuador's Embassy?

We shall fight on the beaches, we shall fight on the landing grounds, we shall fight in the chanceries…

According to Ecuador, the UK embassy in Quito delivered a diplomatic note in mid-August 2012 stating:

You need to be aware that there is a legal base in the UK, the Diplomatic and Consular Premises Act 1987, that would allow us to take actions in order to arrest Mr. Assange in the current premises of the Embassy.

We sincerely hope that we do not reach that point, but if you are not capable of resolving this matter of Mr. Assange's presence in your premises, this is an open option for us.

We need to reiterate that we consider the continued use of the diplomatic premises in this way incompatible with the Vienna Convention and unsustainable and we have made clear the serious implications that this has for our diplomatic relations.

In response, Foreign Minister Ricardo Patino announced, "Today we received from the United Kingdom an express threat, in writing, that they might storm our embassy in London if we don't hand over Julian Assange. Ecuador rejects in the most emphatic terms the explicit threat of the British official communication." Later, in his usual understated manner, President Rafael Correa declared the warning "absolutely unacceptable and a threat to all countries of the world."

So, we can see two options for the British: a) can they indeed "storm" the Ecuadorean embassy; and b) should they?

How to Storm a Foreign Embassy Under International Law

While as a diplomat, I have been arrested, menaced, hassled, harassed and threatened with being made *persona non grata,* I've never had one of my diplomatic missions "stormed," though I've had colleagues who have had. I helped close one embassy (Kabul) that was under serious security threat. I cannot, however, recall my government lifting the diplomatic status of a foreign mission on American soil and then intruding onto the premises. So, can the Brits do it? Wave a magic wand lifting the diplomatic immunity of nine wayward Ecuadorean diplomats and their lilliputian embassy and then send in Scotland Yard to nab one loudmouthed Aussie attention-seeker wanted for sex crimes in Sweden?

British legal expert Carl Gardner (headoflegal.com, August 12, 2012) has looked into his government's stance and has this to say:

The 1987 Act does indeed give ministers a power to withdraw recognition from diplomatic premises. Section 1(3) says

> *In no case is land to be regarded as a State's diplomatic or consular premises for the purposes of any enactment or rule of law unless it has been so accepted or the Secretary of State has given that State consent under this section in relation to it; and if—*

> (a) a State ceases to use land for the purposes of its
> mission or exclusively for the purposes of a consular
> post; or
> (b) the Secretary of State withdraws his acceptance or
> consent in relation to land, it thereupon ceases to be
> diplomatic or consular premises for the purposes of all
> enactments and rules of law.

On the face of it, then, the Secretary of State (in practice a foreign office minister) could now simply withdraw consent, and with one bound, police would be free to make an arrest.

But it's not quite as simple as that. You'll note that section 1(4) says

> The Secretary of State shall only give or withdraw consent or
> withdraw acceptance if he is satisfied that to do so is permissible
> under international law

and that according to section 1(5), in deciding whether to withdraw consent, the minister

> shall have regard to all material considerations, and in particular,
> but without prejudice to the generality of this subsection—
>
> > (a) to the safety of the public;
> > (b) to national security; and
> > (c) to town and country planning.

The "compliance with international law" requirement may present a problem, since article 21 of the Vienna Convention on Diplomatic Relations requires the UK to facilitate the acquisition by Ecuador of *premises necessary for its mission, or assist it in obtaining accommodation. It's not obvious this allows the UK to just de-recognise the current premises without helping arrange something new.*

Section 1(5) is interesting because, in spite of the way the drafting clearly intends to preserve ministers' ability to take account of anything they think relevant, I've no doubt lawyers for Ecuador could argue that the list of three particular concerns colours the scope of ministers' considerations, the result being that only some particular difficulty relating to safety or to the premises themselves could justify withdrawal.

More importantly, they could argue that Assange's presence in the embassy and Ecuador's conduct in sheltering him is not a material consideration; and that since that clearly lay behind the withdrawal, ministers would in deciding to withdraw consent, have taken into account an irrelevant factor.

In addition, there'd be a potentially strong argument to be made that ministers had exercised their power for an improper purpose not intended by Parliament when it enacted the 1987 legislation – their desire to arrest Julian Assange.

Bottom line? As with almost all things legal, it's murky.

Should the United Kingdom Invade the Embassy of a Micro-State Itching for a Fight?

With the legal case about as clear as mud, we turn to the political side. What are the downsides of lifting the diplomatic status of Ecuador's embassy and then sending in law enforcement to arrest Assange? Plenty:

- it makes the Brits look like semi-barbarous bullies
- it puts UK diplomatic missions, especially in Latin America where anti-British sentiments remain strong over the Falklands feud with Argentina, under security threat
- it feeds into the need of tinpot quasi-dictators like Correa and his fellow travelers in Venezuela, Bolivia and now Peru for endless squabbles with Western powers to make themselves look courageous and to divert their people's attention away from domestic problems

In my diplomatic experience, the UK's Foreign and Commonwealth Office (FCO) is one of the most talented and capable foreign ministries in the world. They rarely pursue stupid or unsound policies. Their political leaders, however, may be pushing for a more aggressive policy to get Assange.

So, Just Sever Relations and Kick the Bastards Out

Legal expert Carl Gardner makes the case for the British simply severing diplomatic relations with Ecuador, thus, ridding themselves of an embassy not comporting itself in conformance with international law altogether and thereby grabbing Assange as the lights are turned off after the last diplomat departs:

If I were advising the government, I think I'd say that, if ministers are determined to allow the arrest of Assange, it might be better simply to cut off diplomatic relations with Ecuador, send the ambassador home, close the embassy and arrest Assange after that. Ending diplomatic relations is the major sort of foreign affairs decision I doubt the courts would interfere with. But that'd be a major diplomatic call.

Indeed it is a major diplomatic call. Breaking off diplomatic relations is a big deal. Think U.S.-Cuba, U.S.-Iran, UK-Argentina. This is a last resort act, often accompanied by hostilities. It screws up trade, tourism, travel, communications, banking and a host of other important factors that tie nations together. And if London did break off relations, chances are Ecuador's closest allies might follow suit. British trade with South America, which is significant and growing, could suffer. The resultant damage would far outweigh the ephemeral legal case of one outspoken Aussie loser obsessed with calling constant attention upon himself.

Let Them Stew

Serious thought should be given to a third approach, i.e., the one that London thus far has been following: leave them alone. As I've stated previously, an embassy is not Embassy Suites, particularly a tiny, cramped one like Ecuador's London mission. Over time, Assange and his reluctant local hosts will go stir crazy with each other. The FCO can add to the discomfort by refusing any and all Ecuadorean requests for more space, ease of movement and the other niceties of daily living. Yes, the Latin tinpot madhatters will continue to raise a ruckus, as will Assange's many tinfoil-hatted supporters. Over time, however, the noise will die down. Assange can rail all he wants against "Washington's war on whistle-blowers." But his tirades ring hollow in light of Washington's not issuing, thus far, a formal indictment or request for his extradition. Where's the beef, in other words?

The British are renowned for their patient persistence and judicious reserve. Their best weapon in the Assange case continues to be to stick to the legalities of Sweden's extradition request in connection with Assange's alleged sexual crimes in that country. And let them stew.

ON WRITING

Why I Write

Blowback on a Risky Policy

Ambassador Arnie Raphel, the man who handpicked me to be the State Department's desk officer for Afghanistan, perished in a mysterious plane crash along with Pakistan President Zia ul-Haq in 1988. Thereafter, our policy to oust the Soviets from Afghanistan turned more coldly cynical as we turned a blind eye to our arms support being funneled to radical Islamist fighters. Today we are reaping the consequences as we fight al-Qaeda and the Taliban, heirs of our former no-questions-asked largesse to the Afghans' efforts to end the Soviet occupation.

My Forrest Gump Moment

On November 12, 1986, I was in the West Wing of the White House on official business. After a long meeting, I made a pit stop at the downstairs men's room. While standing doing my business, the door swung open and in streamed several men. At the urinal on my left was Defense Secretary Cap Weinberger. On my right was Secretary of State George Shultz. At the toilet stood CIA Director Bill Casey. They obviously had just come out of a lengthy meeting of their own. All were stonily silent. None acknowledged any of the others. They studiously avoided eye contact at the sink, the towel dispenser and as they sought to exit the room. I sensed a definite chill between them and couldn't wait myself to get out of there. In the outside foyer, a suck-up White House flunky greeted Shultz in a fawning voice. The Secretary stopped in his tracks and, red-faced, glowered at the man, then stormed off.

Next day headlines broke open the Iran-Contra scandal. *The Washington Post* reported on a stormy meeting between Pres. Reagan and his national security officials. For me it was truly a Forrest Gump moment.

Cuban Spies and White House Leakers

I served as the State Department's staff representative to the Cuba Interagency Policy Group in the mid-'90's. This group, chaired by Special Advisor to the President Richard Nuccio, met monthly at the Old Executive Office Building (now the Eisenhower Bldg.) adjacent to the White House; sometimes we convened in the Situation Room in the White House. At this time, I was shuttling to/from Guantanamo Naval Base where I served as the Department's representative to monthly talks with the Cuban military on "The Line" – i.e., the boundary.

The White House group discussed U.S. policies toward Castro's Cuba and tasked the participating agencies with measures to further those policies. Trouble was, sensitive issues were being constantly leaked to the media. It got to the point where some of us became reticent, preferring to do business behind the scenes directly with counterparts in the other agencies. The group itself was sloppily managed, showing little in the way of concrete results.

In late 1996, the CIA stripped Mr. Nuccio of his security clearances. He resigned shortly thereafter. Turns out Mr. Nuccio had been leaking secrets to then Sen. Robert Torricelli and reporters. The investigation also revealed Nuccio had been preparing and transmitting classified documents on his home office equipment. Oh! And Torricelli, caught up in a bribery scandal, left the Senate after one term.

"The fault, dear Brutus, lies not in our stars, but in ourselves."

It wasn't only the press and uncleared members of Congress who were unauthorized recipients of U.S. government secrets about our Cuba policy.

Every month from Guantanamo, I sent classified cables to Washington via U.S. Navy encrypted communications concerning our meetings on The Line with Cuban military representatives as well as on what I'd learned from interviewing Cuban refugees.

When I traveled inside Castro's Cuba on official business, agents of the Cuban intelligence agency, the DGI, followed my every move and harassed me, including slashing the tires of my rental car. While this is standard operating procedure for the DGI, in retrospect, I have to wonder whether Ana Belen Montes may have had something to do with it.

Ana Montes was the U.S. Defense Intelligence Agency's senior analyst for Cuba. She had access to virtually all of our classified intelligence and policy planning on that country. In late 2001, she was arrested for espionage and convicted shortly thereafter. Sentenced to twenty-five years, Ana Montes is imprisoned in Texas.

For sixteen years, Montes had been passing to Castro's intelligence service a veritable torrent of official secrets. Her treason led to the killing of a Green Beret. Had Havana been reading my classified reports in virtual real-time, care of Ana Montes?

███████████ or Keystone Kops?

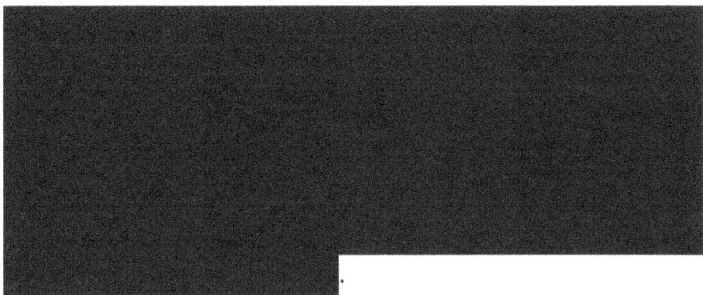

Ambassadors-at-Large for Incompetence...

In 1992, as the Khmer Rouge were targeting foreigners for assassination in the countryside, our ambassador in Cambodia ordered his staff to travel into the lawless interior to ascertain people's attitudes about upcoming UN-sponsored elections for that country. The staff refused such an irresponsible order, confronting the ambassador with passive resistance bordering on insubordination. The State Department countermanded the order.

When working on U.S. policy on Cambodia in the UN in the early '80s, my State Department boss asked me: "Are the Khmer Rouge the good guys or the bad guys?" As most of the world knows, the Khmer Rouge killed at least a million Cambodian citizens in the 1970s, a genocide second only to the Holocaust.

Having just arrived as a young diplomat at an isolated Asian post, my bosses, the Chargé d'Affaires and his deputy, had me accompany them to the home of a wealthy Sino-Thai businessman for luxurious repasts which included delicacies such as shark fin soup, fish maw and barbecued bear paw. This man, however, led a surreptitious life. His entertainment facilities were hidden behind an office bathroom and he dodged all questions about his business and personal life. Suspicious, I sent his name to several U.S. agencies for a database check. The Drug Enforcement Agency promptly replied that our charming dinner host was on their Most Wanted List; he had earlier dropped out of sight, one step ahead of the law. The U.S. Chargé d'Affaires and his staff

had been hobnobbing unawares with a notorious narcotraf-
ficker. Who was dumber: the crook, for entertaining American officials? Or, the clueless officials themselves?

...and Embassies for Sale!

In the late 1980s, our ambassador to Italy was an Italian-
American lumber baron from Minnesota. Having donated
generously to his party, the man got the job, though he
possessed no diplomatic or related experience. An otherwise gregarious sort, he was at sea in Rome. He used one
of the most sensitive communications channels, normally
reserved for matters of high policy, to update the Secretary
of State on his project to remodel Villa Taverna, the U.S.
ambassador's residence, including one lengthy cable on his
selection of curtains. He was also fond of telling demeaning
Italian jokes before crowds of host country officials and
journalists, an act that endeared neither him nor the United
States to the Italian public.

Jimmy Carter's ambassador to Singapore, a former South
Dakota state legislator, walked off with the ambassadorial
china upon completion of his unremarkable assignment.
Upon being asked to return the expensive, eagle-embossed
dinnerware, our ambassador refused, stating it was his just
reward for having been an ambassador.

Faux pas by noncareer ambassadors include cocaine smuggling using diplomatic pouches, drunken imbroglios at
embassy functions, embarrassing adulterous affairs, and
simple ineptitude. We used to sell military flag officer ranks

to political hacks until the end of the Civil War, when the extent of the slaughter revealed the tragic consequences of such practices. U.S. ambassadorships and other senior diplomatic positions, however, remain on the auction block for the highest bidders. Fully a third of ambassadorships, in fact, go to noncareer people.

Let's Kill the Messenger

When Bill Clinton paid a state visit to Vietnam in 2000, the first to a unified Vietnam by a U.S. president, the State Department assigned as presidential interpreter a nice young man whose only interpreting experience theretofore had been at Arlington County Court, where he translated traffic proceedings, family disputes and similar cases. The poor fellow failed miserably, mangling the President's keynote address to the Vietnamese people, and was sent packing on the next plane back to the U.S. I was directed to find a replacement immediately. I did and, lucky for me, he performed magnificently.

Fact Stranger Than Fiction

If you had any illusions that your government is manned with competent, bright, judicious officials who have your best interests at heart, you're wrong. Twenty-five years in the federal government showed me otherwise. Regularly, I faced situations which made me say, "Fiction can't rival this." Our debacle in Iraq, the Mark Foley affair, the Valerie Plame case and the Abramoff scandal only reconfirm my sentiment.

So, I cut short my diplomatic career to have more fun writing stories which encompass the chicanery and fecklessness of government. If you thought Washington was out of control, then don't read my books. They'll only confirm your worst fears about how things are done in our nation's capital. My spy-mob thriller *Permanent Interests* and *CHASM*, a thriller about war criminals, have landed simultaneously on three Amazon Kindle Bestseller lists, including #1 in Political Fiction and Spy Stories. They were joined by *Tribe*, a political thriller centered on Afghanistan. *Havana Queen*, an espionage thriller set in Cuba is newly released.

What It Takes to Be a Fiction Writer

Poetry is the spontaneous overflow of powerful feelings: it takes its origin from emotion recollected in tranquillity.
~ William Wordsworth.

When I was four, new neighbors moved into the old farmhouse next to us. They had three kids in the same age range as my siblings and me. Redheaded, frecklefaced Eddy came to introduce himself and to play. I hit Eddy in the head with a brick. Since that time, I've always felt more comfortable being a brick-throwing iconoclast than as a team player.

In her hilarious essay on writing, *Bird By Bird*, Anne Lamott confides that when she was a kid she "was very clearly the one who was going to grow up to be a serial killer, or keep dozens and dozens of cats." I believe that the best fiction writers are the nonconformists, the round peg in the square hole types who spend their productive lives building up resentments, hang-ups, broken romances, a few good friendships, off the wall ideas, a healthy and justifiable tinge of paranoia and unfettered dreams when everyone else is collaborating with each other to produce flow charts and financial plans. Those who cruise through life being the teacher's pet, winning awards, marrying the team captain and generally fitting in tend to be lousy fiction writers. They may get straight A's on their English class assignments, but they lack the scarred bark that covers the surfaces of the souls of misfits. Think of the clubfooted Lord Byron and the consumptive Edgar Allan Poe, both oddballs who wrote brilliantly and died young.

I'll make another confession. When I was at the U.S. Naval War College, I spent as much time plotting and writing my first novel as I did studying Clausewitz and fleet configuration during wartime. While my fellow officers went off after classes to crash on term papers, analyze the Peloponnesian Wars or sail their skiffs in beautiful Narragansett Bay, I ensconced myself in a far rear corner of the computer room and conjured my story of powerful evildoers, tragic romance, intrigue, danger and courage while Keith Jarrett played through the headphones. Conditions were set for a spontaneous overflow of emotions recollected in tranquility. My political thriller *Permanent Interests* was therefore conceived with the help of the U.S. Navy. Go Navy! An instructor or fellow student would occasionally inquire about my spending hours by myself typing away madly in that stark room. I would mumble something about working on a paper concerning nuclear strategy or combined arms tactics in littoral conditions. As class president and senior ranking member, I had appearances to keep up.

I graduated somewhere in the upper middle of my class, much to the expressed disappointment of senior staff. Better was expected of an Ivy Leaguer placed in senior training for a fast track career, all expenses borne by Uncle Sam. I'm afraid my budding alternate career as a novelist clearly detracted from my work as an adult student, something I obviously couldn't tell them. *But!* The upside was that the first publisher I'd queried wanted my manuscript! After that I got an agent! Then another one! Then another! Then I got published and *Permanent Interests* made onto three Amazon bestseller lists and mostly stayed there for over a year, along with *CHASM*.

My stories portray Washington power players in authentic settings, exercising levers of power genuinely described. But their motivations are depicted through an Alice in Wonderland looking glass: amply warped and off center. Henry James said "a writer is a person on whom nothing is lost." Hence, the fine detail I bring to bear on the White House, Pentagon, CIA, State Department and the way they do things. I believe readers relish this kind of authenticity. That's a key reason they're buying my books in record numbers that continue to climb.

This oddball who finds it much more fun to throw bricks than to build with them certainly deserves, but also relishes, the splendid isolation that a writing career provides. Few people are cut out for such a lonely undertaking. So, it's okay to return to your flow charts. But if the bark on your soul is scarred, and you've always felt like the odd man/woman out, you just might make a fine fiction writer. Just ask Georgie Byron and Eddy Poe.

BTW, my neighbor Eddy became a best friend. I never clobbered him again.

Inspired Insomniac: Voices in the Dark

Listen to them - the children of the night. What music they make!
~ Bram Stoker, *Dracula*

My most productive writing comes after the sun goes down. Like some manic ghoul, I type madly away, becoming more inspired as the moon rises and the sky blackens. I routinely write until 3:00 am every evening. If I'm on a roll, I'll stretch it out till 4:00 or 4:30. I come to life at night. Somewhere in the family tree, there's no doubt vampire blood.

This routine started out as necessity. Working at the State Department or at one of our overseas missions, of course, I was tied to an 8:15-5:30 (more like 8:15-7:00, or later) schedule. Right after dinner, I'd lock myself away and write and get as much in as possible before midnight. On weekends and holidays, I'd let myself go and succumb to my inherent vampire ways. I owe much to Newt Gingrich. His shutting down the government in late '96 - early '97 gave me a precious, uninterrupted month to crash on my first novel, *Permanent Interests*. I also grew a beard and dressed every day like a fugitive from justice. My wife at first was indulgent, then less and less so as my appearance descended into that of a character from *Deliverance*. Oh, men!

"All profound things and emotions of things are preceded and attended by Silence," wrote Herman Melville. One imagines that Captain Ahab and the great white whale were spawned in a swale of silence as Melville, too, literally burnt the midnight oil to produce his masterpieces of fiction. But the silence of the marketplace threw him into a three-decade funk. His unfinished *Billy Budd*, which he was working on at the time of his death, wasn't published until thirty-three years later.

But silence is what motivates this writer. The silence of the night, when most living things retreat to slumber, provides the uninterrupted peace of mind to create new worlds. Like "creatures of the night," my story characters emerge from the darkness that surrounds me. They command my undivided attention, talk to me about how they plot against each other, flirt, face danger and let their emotions run rampant. I listen to them and, like a deviant court stenographer, chronicle their exploits, their frustrations, their loves, their ambitions – both realized and smitten. The beautiful Russian courtesan, Lydia, jumps out to tell me of her travails at the mercy of powerful men in *Permanent Interests*. The ex-East German Stasi agent, Horst Fechtmann in *CHASM*, explains to me that he turned to free-lance killing only as a means to comfortably retire in Key West as proprietor of his own fern bar. Society doyenne Camilla Loomis, of *Tribe*, pleads with me to understand why she had to conceal her trailer trash origins as she clawed her way to the top of the Washington political structure. And Yuri, alias Captain Zero in *Havana Queen*, ruthlessly slaughtered Castro's minions, he says, only because they imprisoned and tortured his father and, besides, all revolutions are born in blood. These characters get under my skin, go to bed with me, and keep talking to me throughout the day. After the sun goes down and the world falls silent, I then record their tales.

The Spanish have a saying, *Quién a solas se ríe, de sus maldades se acuerda.* "He who laughs when he is alone is remembering his evil deeds." A family member who slipped downstairs for a nocturnal glass of milk in my house might overhear me cackling in the solitude of my study. In the stroke of a laptop key, I may have mercilessly killed off a bad guy, or sent a corrupt politician to prison, or cuckolded a megalomaniacal plutocrat. Sometimes the affected character is taken whole cloth from my past: a wicked boss, a conceited high official, a crass military officer, a testicle-crushing ambition-crazed female colleague. In this way, writing is therapy. Do in your fantasy world what you are barred from doing in the real world – and tell the whole world about it as people buy and read your books.

So, it is 2:30 in the morning as I write this and, believe it or not, the moon is full. So, if you'll excuse me, I must attend to my characters. They are clamoring for my attention.

Why Spies Love My Books

A former CIA officer going under the alias of "Max Cool" said this of *Tribe* in his Amazon review:

As a retired officer of the CIA's Clandestine Service, I was particularly struck by the verisimilitude of his renditions of the confusing and ambiguous life of the intelligence officer in the field, and the maddening and obtuse ways of intelligence bureaucrats at headquarters…and he describes them here in vivid color and accurate detail. His descriptions are so good I wondered at times how he got them through the government reviewers…If you like fast-paced adventure, an ingenious story, and good writing, read Tribe.

In his review of *Permanent Interests*, a Pentagon official stated:

I would make this book required reading for many undergraduate and graduate courses in foreign affairs or national security, and hope that it becomes familiar to the students at our service war colleges in Newport, Carlisle, and Maxwell Air Force Base.

The book review site Reader's Favorite commented:

It is clear the author has first-hand experience of the novel's politics and his encyclopedic knowledge of the turmoil of the Middle East and Afghanistan is impressive.

An early reviewer of my Cuba thriller, *Havana Queen*, stated:

James Bruno's career rivals that of Indiana Jones.

New York Times bestselling author Gloria Nagy stated:

Bruno's detailed depictions of espionage tradecraft lend added drama to his story while revealing an in-depth knowledge of this dark art.

And a State Department diplomat said in his review of *CHASM*:

He uses his insider's knowledge of Washington's power corridors to make the whole yarn come frighteningly to life.

National security professionals love my books because they are the most authentic spy fiction on the market. They read thrillers with a close eye to detail and verisimilitude and they love it when they're reading the genuine article as opposed to the usual contrived spy thriller fantasies. Intel officers, in particular, are expert in separating reality from b.s. In my books, they see only the former. Unless they've worked on the inside like myself, even the best spy thriller writers can only approximate real life espionage and national security workings in their books. Most don't even come close. This is why British ex-spy John LeCarré has been so successful for so long. He gets it right. And so do I.

Each of my novels has undergone a rigorous security review by the U.S. government prior to publication. These reviews take around six months as the manuscript is distributed to various national security agencies for scrubbing to ensure I don't leak any secrets. *Tribe* underwent text redactions and modifications required by the CIA and the FBI. The State Department and a highly secret intelligence agency were a bit less onerous. The upshot is you get the most genuine espionage and diplomacy rendered in fiction this side of Wikileaks.

Foremost in the censors' minds is protecting "sources and methods." One hears this a lot inside the intelligence community. It refers to the ways and means of obtaining intelligence, whether by old fashioned human spycraft or by advanced technical means such as spy satellites. To ensure I continue to get it right, I have my own expanding personal network of "sources and methods." As I state in the Acknowledgements of *Tribe*,

I extend heartfelt thanks to my friends and colleagues in the intelligence community, who choose to remain anonymous, for their insights into espionage tradecraft, thus, lending added authenticity to my story.

"Max Cool" goes on to say,

Bruno is a diplomat who served in some of the most difficult and interesting posts the U.S. Foreign Service has – where intrigue, excitement, and weirdness mix with the lobotomizing effects of government bureaucracy.

This is another key element which makes my writing more genuine than that of other thriller writers. I knew Afghan President Hamid Karzai when we was a mere political operative in the Afghan resistance to Soviet occupation. I also dealt with many of the mujahidin commanders who now lead the Taliban. I worked shoulder-to-shoulder with Secret Service agents in a protective detail for President and Mrs. Clinton. I carried out diplomacy with Cambodia's King Sihanouk. I've spent ample time in the White House, including the West Wing. I've either been in forums with or met five U.S. presidents. I met repeatedly with Cuban military and intelligence officers for discussions on "The Line" at Guantanamo Naval Base. I've also been surveilled and harassed by the intelligence services of at least six nations. I've worked closely with all U.S. national security agencies. I'm a graduate of the U.S. Naval War College. And I've spent more time than I care to recall in various war zones and mine fields. I draw on this wealth of experience in crafting my fiction.

If you peruse the reviews of my books on Amazon, you'll see that they are overwhelmingly favorable. And this has paid off in my books being Amazon Kindle bestsellers. If real spies love them, so will you. You won't be disappointed.

Writing About Spies: Some Observations

A spy, like a writer, lives outside the mainstream population. He steals his experience through bribes and reconstructs it.
~ John LeCarré.

I am often asked, "Why do you write about spies? Were you one yourself?" To answer the last question, no, I never worked as a spy, though I did work briefly as an analyst in military intelligence prior to joining the Foreign Service as a young man. I write about spies and espionage simply because it's sexier than writing about bland diplomats who play by the rules. Spies conceal their true identities and steal secrets through bribes mainly. Diplomats chat it up with their counterparts at boring cocktail receptions, then retreat to their offices to write up dry dispatches to their foreign office or ministry about what they heard. The Austrian satirist Karl Kraus said, "How is the world ruled and how do wars start? Diplomats tell lies to journalists and then believe what they read."

[redacted]. When dating my to-be wife, a British female friend described me, to my chagrin, as "the perfect son-in-law."

[redacted] Diplomats court, spies break hearts. Spies are the bad boys, the rakes, the rule-breakers. There's something about the outlaw that fascinates people, draws them to them. Images of James Bond come to mind. Sexy and dangerous.

Anything but.

"What the hell do you think spies are? Moral philosophers measuring everything they do against the word of God or Karl Marx? They're not! They're just a bunch of seedy, squalid bastards like me: little men, drunkards, queers, hen-pecked husbands, civil servants playing cowboys and Indians to brighten their rotten little lives." So said LeCarré character Alec Leamas in The Spy Who Came in From the Cold.

and from my spy thriller, *Tribe*...

"Past this point lies a hermetically sealed inner world of secretive bureaucrats who labor intensely in office cubicles swathed in ice-white fluorescence. Only the push-button combination locks on office doors, ubiquitous safes and occasional special access control units in corridors distinguish this place from a zillion other unremarkable office warrens of insurance companies, state agencies or computer conglomerates. This includes the workers, mostly sporting department store suits and shopping mall haircuts. Serious, sexless, sober people with a passion not to stand out."

"I stare at this man. I wonder now as I have every day for the past twenty years how is it that they allow such little men to play God with other people's lives. Middle-class, suburban super-functionaries who shop for grass seed on Sunday and smuggle rocket-propelled grenade launchers to tribals on Monday."

In my quarter-century-long government career, none of the spies I knew were charismatic swashbucklers. The vast majority were family men and women, with a liberal sprinkling of alcoholics, sex-addicted, and mildly nutso characters. Most worried about making their mortgage payments and getting their kids into the gifted program just like the rest of us. And most complained about the straitjacket of red tape that ties up the professional lives of all government functionaries.

Serious spies work hard and laboriously at their tradecraft. Ex-CIA officer Valerie Plame is an example of a serious, sober professional who built a knowledge base on nuclear proliferation brick by brick while serving for years under deep "nonofficial cover" until the Vice President and his evil minions outed her. Russian SVR "illegal" Russian spy Anna Chapman, on the other hand, comported herself like a Gen-X party girl with tradecraft more attuned to a three-ring circus than to the gray world of spies.

The allure and mystique of espionage is what people like to read about. So, I draw on my personal experiences, meticulous open-source research and the insights of anonymous sources in the intelligence community to spin out tales that keep the reader guessing and tsk-tsking and shaking their head while, at the same time, grinning mischievously and wanting more.

Writing the National Security Thriller, Tips for the Lay Author, Part I

Two ingredients are essential for writing a successful novel: good writing and knowledge of the subject matter. Just as a murder mystery reads better when the detective work and forensics reflect true life, so is it with national security thrillers. These include spy, political and military thrillers.

Verisimilitude: Separating the Plausible from the B.S.

What separates the outstanding national security thrillers from the rest of the pack is verisimilitude: creating characters, situations and plots that closely resemble the real thing. The worst thrillers are the ones where the author simply fabricates how a spy/political actor/soldier operates. That is not to say that the latter don't become bestsellers. They often do. The authors of thrillers lacking in verisimilitude succeed by spinning a good yarn for which readers are willing to suspend big-time disbelief. Ian Fleming's James

Bond is a case in point. Wonderful entertainment. Totally divorced from the real world.

I've lost count of how many mega bestselling thrillers I've quit reading because I just couldn't buy into the authors' story premise, character, methods or goals. I put down one bestselling thriller author's book after reading that her young protagonist was a CIA superstar agent after being active for only one year and who had an aversion to weapons. This author also refers to the CIA as "The Company," a term that fell out of use by the early '70s. This isn't bad research; it reflects no research at all. Just pulling a story out of her ear. Likewise, I aborted two other bestsellers by another thriller writer after getting fed up with endless numbers of jaws being kicked in and cars cracked up. The stories are more befitting comic books than novels.

Three living authors whose thrillers excel in large part due to their close adherence to how the real spy world operates are John LeCarré, Daniel Silva and David Ignatius. LeCarré gets it right because he himself was a spy in Her Majesty's service. Silva and Ignatius get it right by developing reliable sources who are or were intelligence officers and by doing careful, methodical research, drawing on their journalistic training. They know their settings intimately, having worked in the countries in which their stories take place. LeCarré is expert at capturing the banality of the spy bureaucracy. Their characters are conflicted operators in a gray world of uncertain morality; no comic book heroes performing fantastical feats on the side of righteousness in bogus settings.

Among the critical praise that I value most highly for my writing is that from a retired CIA officer who wrote of my thriller, *Tribe*: "I was particularly struck by the verisimilitude of his renditions of the confusing and ambiguous life of the intelligence officer in the field, and the maddening and obtuse ways of intelligence bureaucrats at headquarters… His descriptions are so good I wondered at times how he got them through the government reviewers."

Getting It Right

So, how do you get it right if you've never worked as a government agent or prize-winning national security correspondent? By doing your research:

- First, constantly read the wealth of nonfiction books about the espionage world to get a good grip on jargon, procedures, tradecraft and bureaucracy. These include as well books by investigative journalists on specific cases: the Walker spy ring, the Aldrich Ames, Robert Hanssen, Ana Montes, Jonathan Pollard and other cases.
- Second, dive into the news archives on such cases. One recent and rare motherlode of information on so-called "illegals" or "sleeper agents" is the reporting on the ten deep cover Russian spies caught recently in the U.S. posing as American citizens. Books will certainly follow the news reporting.
- Third, try to develop sources among acquaintances, friends and family members who have professional experience in intelligence, diplomacy, law

enforcement, etc. Ask them if you could pick their minds on how things are actually done in their respective fields.

- Another often overlooked source of nitty-gritty information is court indictments. Reading the indictments on Hanssen, Ames, Montes and the Russian sleepers is a real eye-opener on spy tradecraft. These can be either googled, or obtained from the websites of the regional U.S. Attorney offices which prosecuted given cases.

When writing your thriller, you can create a structure based on real cases, then fill it in with your fictitious characters and story line. The impact on the reader will be positive. You will be viewed as a writer who knows his/her stuff, a real authority.

The Craft: No Amateurs Need Apply

The flip side of the coin on being a honed national security thriller writer is, of course, talent. You can have worked as a legendary spy for thirty years, but if you haven't the foggiest notion of character, voice, plotting, structure, conflict, pacing, etc., it's best not to waste your time or that of potential readers by trying to slap together something resembling a novel when you lack grounding in the craft of fiction writing. There's the retired intelligence officer whose nonfiction books have been well received, but whose sole novel falls flat because the author lacks any such grounding. His story flops around for three-hundred pages; his protagonist is repulsive; the plot is missing in action. A reviewer said of this author, "he has the hallmarks of someone who has a driver's license, but who has been asked to fly a plane. The result is a dead-on crash, no survivors." The lesson: Know the subject matter. Know the craft. Without both, you'll either fail as a novelist or open yourself to serious criticism for not knowing your subject matter.

Writing the National Security Thriller: Tips for the Lay Author, Part II: People, Places & Things

In my first installment on writing the national security thriller, I stressed the importance of verisimilitude in one's story. The thrillers which exert the greatest hold on the reader's imagination are those that mimic real life, but are nonetheless bigger than life. The *Die Hard* movie series starring Bruce Willis is so successful because of this, as well as Willis's everyman character, John McClane. Contrast this with the Terminator series, starring Arnold Schwarzenegger, also hugely successful. But the latter is a science fiction thriller; its verisimilitude is not tied so much to current-day real life and requires a greater suspension of disbelief, which is part and parcel of the science fiction genre. If you're writing political, spy or military thrillers, it's best to stick to getting your facts right as you weave them into your tale of fictitious persons and events.

People: Composite or Wholecloth?

For my political thriller, *Tribe*, I wanted to populate the story with bigger-than-life, memorable characters whom the reader would either love or loathe. So, I chose genuine political actors, real folks who cast a big shadow during their days in the sun of political power. These people, some of whom I had known personally, were better material than I could dream up in my own fertile imagination. Big egos, big appetites, big mouths, big influence. I simply couldn't make them up and I wanted them in my story. Truth indeed is stranger than fiction. But then, as with most things in life, we run up against the lawyers: *any resemblance to actual persons, living or dead, business establishments, events, or locales is entirely coincidental.* Remember libel, slander? Oh yeah. That. Well. Let's just change the names and a few other details, then slap on that legalese boilerplate to keep us out of court-induced penury or the hoosegow.

So, my "Robert Norfolk," an egomaniacal, loud-mouthed power player and inveterate womanizer, blithe-ly wrecks careers and countries in his clamber to the top. My socialite "Camilla Loomis" uses people and discards them in her own quest up the D.C. power ladder. An assortment of Afghan jihadis and warlords bear an uncanny resemblance to people you may have read about in books or newspapers. Senior CIA officers in *Tribe* may remind some government officials of people they actually know. Hmm. One reviewer described my characters as "the most believable Washing-ton political villains you've ever witnessed dissembling on the news talk shows." The upshot: some characters are less composite than others.

I read tomes of biographies and took copious notes. I watched old news clips of the people I was researching. I consulted individuals who had worked for or known them. It wasn't long that they took up a life of their own in my imagination. As I stated in my essay, *Inspired Insomniac: Voices in the Dark*, "These characters get under my skin, go to bed with me, and keep talking to me throughout the day. After the sun goes down and the world falls silent, I then record their tales."

The key thing about fashioning characters after real life actors is that the latters' lives in politics, espionage, military, law enforcement, what-have-you are recorded in detail. So, Camilla Loomis's real life doppelganger's Georgetown house, her parties, her horse farm, her way of getting what she wanted are all there in her biographies and news coverage. Same goes for Robert Norfolk's self-centered machinations or that CIA Director's covering his ass. Crib liberally from real life players. Change some details. Slap on your character's name – and don't forget to top it off with that *any resemblance to actual persons* caveat at the beginning of your book. There's nothing like drawing on the lives of real people to create verisimilitude in your story.

Places: What Does Sanaa Smell Like?

Many thriller writers may have some international travel under their belts, but probably not in Kandahar, Kinshasa or Kaliningrad. As a diplomat, I can draw on a host of exotic locales I've been to, but I haven't been everywhere. I was fortunate to be able to write in three-dimensional detail about the Afghanistan-Pakistan border areas where I've served. But for the climactic scene where my protagonist rescues his daughter from Islamist kidnappers in Yemen, I was lost. Never been there. So, I researched everything I could about present-day Yemen from online and other sources, including guidebooks. But it wasn't enough. I didn't have the fingerspitzgefuhl I always demand when describing a place. What does Sanaa sound and smell like? How do people carry out their daily lives? What is sold in the markets? What arms are sold in Yemen's Wild East gun bazaars? What are some common Yemeni expressions? What's the national narcotic-chaw, *qat*, taste like? etc., etc.

I consulted some good travelogue websites. They were exceedingly valuable. One travel blog by a young British student who was studying Arabic in Yemen particularly caught my eye. The writer was acerbic, funny and detail-focused. So, I emailed him, explained I was a novelist and could use his insights for my latest thriller. He was delighted to help out. He answered all of my questions and offered more descriptions of Yemen and Yemenis, detailed info I wasn't getting from elsewhere. As a result, I was able to place my characters in a Yemen that the reader can find highly credible, thus enhancing the verisimilitude of place. A *New York Times* bestselling author who reviewed *Tribe* commented, "The action in exotic locales like Central Asia and the Arabian Peninsula has an eyewitness feel to it." This is what a thriller writer lives for (after high sales volume, of course). I mentioned the student's name in my Acknowledgements section and sent him a free copy of the book.

I draw on my service in Cuba and at Guantanamo Naval Base heavily in my thriller, *Havana Queen*. But I left Cuba in the late '90s and haven't been back. I needed to be up-to-date. I read a pile of recent books and travel articles. But I needed more. I hadn't realized that Cuba has a very active blogosphere, the most interesting being those of political dissidents and human rights activists. The most informative and entertaining is that of prominent dissident-blogger Yoani Sanchez. With wit and irony, she describes life of Cubans inside their own country with great insight. What kinds of permits are needed to travel, to open a restaurant? How do people spread word about events, domestic and foreign, which the Communist party deems verboten? How does one scrape together groceries each day in a country saddled with shortages of just about everything, including tropical fruit, of all things? Yoani fills in the gaps and then some, as do her fellow bloggers. Fascinating stuff, and great input for the novelist.

But, if you've never been to Cuba, or GTMO, how do you describe them? Ahh! Another miracle of the internet age: Google Earth. When I worked in government pre-internet, one required a top secret clearance to view satellite photos of other countries. Now, I can zoom into downtown Havana, or Santiago or GTMO with the flick of a finger in my armchair at home. Wanna know what "The Line" – Cuba's Checkpoint Charlie where I used to meet with Cuban military officers – looks like? Google Earth takes you there. Amazing! The only serious limitation to the thriller writer's utilizing these tools is his/her own descriptive skills.

A vignette: I had a tussle with CIA censors when getting *Tribe* security reviewed. In chapter six, I described a place containing a widely known government facility. CIA nixed it. I then faxed them extracts from published books – plus links to Google Earth showing it in great detail. So, what's the fuss, I asked? They stood their ground and I lost that battle anyway. Win some, lose some.

So, with due diligence, anyone can get granular detail on virtually every square inch of this planet. All it takes is honed research skills.

Things: AK-47 or AK-74?

How many thrillers have you read in which an assassin or the hero just shoots bad guys? Was he using a Glock or a blunderbuss? Who knows? For this reader, lack of detail detracts from the credibility of the story. And, if gunning down terrorists, which is better: the AK-47 or the AK-74? (No, this is not a typo.) It's useful to know which. In the case of the AK's, the former uses a bigger round than the latter. A bigger round cuts clean through a body, while a smaller caliber bullet wreaks bloody havoc to a human corpus. How about close-in assassination? And what if your killer came from the former East Bloc? You can give him a Colt-45, but many of your cognoscenti-readers will be groaning. Many of my readers are current or former military and intelligence people. They love verisimilitude. So, I make sure my ex-East German Stasi assassin in *CHASM*, Horst Fechtmann, whacks his targets with weapons he grew up with professionally: Makarov or Glock pistols, and the Dragunov sniper rifle. How do I know this? I researched it in *Jane's Military Review* and other obscure tomes of forgotten lore. There are also plenty of online resources. And don't forget the Military Channel on cable TV; it's a wealth of very useful visual information.

BTW, Sanaa smells like spices, diesel exhaust and cat piss.

Writing the National Security Thriller, Part III: Spy Tradecraft

In my first two articles on Writing the National Security Thriller, I addressed the importance of verisimilitude and people, places and things. But the heart of any espionage tale lies in spy tradecraft. If the writing is good, the plot appears true-to-life and you've populated your story with credible characters, places and things, and you've got the tradecraft nailed down, you at least have the makings of a winner.

When I worked as a diplomat in Cuba, that country's intelligence services were on me practically 24/7. They tailed me constantly, riffled through my belongings, slashed my car tires, bugged my phone calls and placed hidden videocams in my hotel rooms. In Vietnam, that country's intelligence service set up a clandestine surveillance post in a building just opposite my villa and kept watch on me and my family for four years. I was often tailed there as well. Same in China, Laos and Cambodia. The formerly communist Hungarian secret service tried to lure me into a so-called "honey trap." I got into a car chase with a Russian KGB agent who pissed me off, and required 24/7 armed bodyguards in face of Iranian threats to U.S. diplomats. State

Department Diplomatic Security authorized me to carry a weapon at times like that after scoring top marks in shooting tests. I also had the privilege of once working with the Secret Service on a presidential protection detail. All great grist for my novels.

When you serve as a U.S. envoy in countries ruled by governments hostile to America, these types of things become almost second nature. I incorporate my real-life experiences with intelligence and security activities in my thrillers. But what if the Cuban Directorate of Intelligence hasn't been on your case? And what if the Iranians haven't issued a fatwa against you? What if (for you) "Walk-ins Welcome" means your hairdresser accepts customers with no appointments rather than (to me) political defectors are encouraged to join our side? If you're an insurance adjuster by day, but an aspiring thriller writer in your free time, what do you do to make your tales crackle with authentic action as opposed to lumbering under contrived artifice? Ask Tom Clancy. He pulled it off and the rest is history.

There's no easy route to enlightenment here. Research and more research is the answer. Before even thinking of setting fingertips to keyboard with your story, hit the books and gain an understanding of the arcane worlds of espionage, or the military, or politics, or law enforcement, or whatever niche in which you're writing. As for espionage, I recommend reading the works of the best spy thriller fiction writers: John LeCarré, Eric Ambler, Alan Furst, Daniel Silva, David Ignatius. Other spy tale writers may slap together entertaining yarns, but too many of them flunk the reality test. I'd avoid them as I researched for my own opus and stick to the masters.

On the non-fiction side, there are surprisingly few classic guides on spy tradecraft. Two that I recommend (if you can find them in print) are: *The Craft of Intelligence* by Allen Dulles and *Without Cloak or Dagger: The Truth About the New Espionage* by Miles Copeland. They provide the timeless basics of spy tradecraft in very readable form. Another good, but more up-to-date, introduction is Wikipedia. Start with their article on HUMINT, i.e., human intelligence: *http://en.wikipedia.org/wiki/Clandestine_HUMINT*. And, as I stated in my last article on writing the national security thriller, read the many excellent nonfiction books, usually by journalists, on real spy cases – the Walker spy ring, Aldrich Ames, Robert Hansson, Jonathan Pollack, Ana Montes, et al. They provide detailed accounts of how spies, traitors and counterspies work. Finally, another good source on tradecraft is the legal indictments against those caught spying for foreign powers – all of the above cases plus the Russian sleeper agent ring cracked by the FBI in 2010. These documents can be found through the websites of the relevant U.S. Attorney offices which prosecuted the cases.

If you invest the time poring over all of these resources, you'll find yourself actually grasping the esoteric and twisted world of spies and how they operate. You'll also find yourself doing surveillance detection runs in your hometown just in case the Cuban DI is on your case…

Zero Dark Thirty, Homeland, Argo and the Art of Verisimilitude

In the hit TV series *Homeland,* Nicholas Brody bears the rank of Gunnery Sergeant on his service uniform but his dress blues show him to be only a Sergeant, and he is addressed throughout as "Sergeant" rather than "Gunnery Sergeant" (or "Gunny"). In the movie *Argo,* the U.S. embassy Marine guards are wearing Battle Dress Uniforms (BDU). BDUs were not introduced until the fall of 1981. *Zero Dark Thirty's* protagonist Maya repeatedly refers to *"Pesh-*awar," a city in Pakistan; its proper pronunciation is Pesh-*a*-war, something a CIA analyst working there certainly would know.

A self-admitted nerd-wonk, I'm addicted to good political fiction. Like many others, I'm glued to *Homeland,* and recently saw *Argo* and *Zero Dark Thirty.* One would think that, after two-and-a-half decades of coughing Pushtunistan dust, negotiating through Southeast Asian minefields, dodging Cuban agents, and suffering under life-sucking government bureaucracy, I'd prefer tango dancing or building a wine cellar or something else approaching normal. But I'm a writer who writes what he knows and what I know is anything but normal: tribal politics (American as well as foreign), intrigue, weapons, spies, and the arcane art of diplomacy.

I go to great lengths in my own books to get my facts right -- does the Rashid assault rifle use the standard AK 7.62mm round? (Yes). On what side street is Cuba's spy agency? (Calle 19). What is the name of the CIA's main training facility? (sorry, they made me take that one out - really!). I bring this anal-retentiveness along with a bag of popcorn with me to the cinema. I'm one of those insufferable types who'll keep a running commentary going while the show is on.

Anyway, to make the most impact on viewing audiences, movie producers need to get their facts straight. Taking dramatic license is fine. Making lots of factual errors is not. I wrote about this in my three-part series, "Writing the National Security Thriller." Let's compare the three Hollywood productions in question:

In *Argo*, producer Ben Affleck has done a magnificent job of recreating a 1970s atmosphere, right down to borrowing footage of busy office scenes from *All the President's Men* to portray CIA headquarters and recreating Iranian uniforms from the period. I'd written previously about his accurate depiction of diplomats under siege and the tension of planning escape from a volatile revolutionary setting. He also captures well the bureaucratic tension in Washington as State Department and White House officials hesitate to give the green light for such a risky rescue operation. Affleck, on the other hand, has caught serious flak over his demeaning the central roles played by the Canadian, British, New Zealand and other governments in assisting the hostages. And he takes dramatic license in the totally fictional scenes of the hostages, under cover as Canadian film makers, touring a bazaar; and the white-knuckle airport getaway.

I was disappointed by the many factual errors in *Zero Dark Thirty*, which, I felt, detracted somewhat from an otherwise gripping production. Mispronouncing Peshawar is one of a number of basic errors that could easily have been avoided had the producers simply consulted some experts. They apparently did receive some CIA cooperation, a matter some senators have called to be investigated. The CIA analyst Maya (Jessica Chastain) tells CIA chief Panetta (played by James Gandolfini) that she was recruited right out of high school. Agency analysts and case officers are not recruited out of high school, and almost all have at least a B.A. degree. In a chase scene in "Pakistan," an Indian flag is clearly visible in the background, betraying the film location in Chandigarh, India. For some mysterious reason, they cast a Brit speaking UK English in the role of National Security Advisor Thomas Donilon. The mistake that drew a big guffaw from me was the Islamabad CIA station chief's sporting a CIA logo pin on his lapel like a bullseye over his heart. This little touch is just downright stupid. The COS's later sporting an American flag lapel pin, while not impossible, is highly unlikely. One just doesn't see this kind of patriotism-on-one's-sleeve affectation among career officials. And, of course, there is the controversy over whether torture was used to track down bin-Laden. CIA Director Morell stated, "That impression is false. We cannot allow a Hollywood film to cloud our memory." Former CIA counterterrorism officer Nada Bakos concluded, *Zero Dark Thirty* is "not accurate enough to resonate with my experiences as a CIA analyst and later, a targeting officer in the clandestine service."

With the exception of some dramatic license, *Homeland* displays the most care in adhering to real life intelligence and counterterrorism work, right down to the nuances of policies and regulations. Carrie (Claire Danes) conceals her bipolar disorder, including filching her meds rather than getting a doctor to prescribe them. Why? Because her employer likely would pull her clearances, a career death knell. This kind of thing really happens (see "Running Amok: Mental Health in the U.S. Foreign Service"). Saul's (Mandy Patinkin) wife splitting with him because his career consumes his life is very familiar to people who work in that business. The bureaucratic lingo is accurate and current. So is the attire, right down to Saul's department store officewear. The bureaucratic procedures, egos and dumbassedness are genuine. It is clear that this series's producers rely heavily on former CIA and military people as resources to get their story straight. On the other hand, a CIA officer (Carrie) carrying out a rogue surveillance operation against an American citizen (Brody) on American soil -- with her supervisor's assent, no less -- is simply unrealistic unless all concerned had no compunction about landing a long prison sentence. But, of the three thrillers, *Homeland* gets two thumbs up from this observer for authenticity and adherence to detail.

Verisimilitude is what the thriller writer should aim for when concocting a story, be it cinematic, television or literary. Say *Pesh*-awar enough times, wear a CIA logo pin, mix up uniforms and get the jargon wrong and you'll lose some respect among the cognoscenti at least. Get it right, and you've got a winner.

P.S. Hollywood producers: I'm available as an expert consultant at reasonable rates.

Why I'm Censored

"Congress shall make no law. . .abridging the freedom of speech, or of the press."

"Where art thou, Faustus? Wretch, what hast thou done?

Damn'd art thou, Faustus, damn'd!"

A Pact With the Devil

When I signed up as a Foreign Service officer of the United States and again when I signed out twenty-three years later, I had to agree in writing to official censorship of anything I wrote prior to publication, and all public speaking before presentation. Thus, unlike the rest of the American population, I do not enjoy the full freedoms of expression covered in the Constitution. Alas, I made a faustian pact with Uncle Sam, who owns the creative part of my soul unto death. In return, he paid me to travel and live in exotic lands, gave me fancy titles, provided me with adventure and even romance sometimes, and made me privy to the innermost secrets of state. And he protects the latter zealously.

Where's G. Gordon Liddy When We Need Him?

Uncle Sam hates leaks. But like the enchanted broom in Disney's Fantasia, he scrambles from pillar to post trying to stem a veritable torrent of secrets, exposés, scandals and slips. And, like the sorcerer's apprentice, he finds it to be overwhelming and largely futile. Witness the case of Wikileaks. The worst offenders, ironically, are rarely the career lifers like myself, but rather those who direct the beast from within its belly: the political appointees who spin, smear and self-promote as a matter of course; those for whom the rules don't really apply, even when they're caught. And when they are, a sacrificial lamb is thrown to the wolves to protect the higher-ups: viz., Oliver North, Lewis Libby. Karl Rove and Dick Cheney outed CIA undercover officer Valerie Plame, yet never spent a minute in court to answer for their crimes.

In my time in the State Department, this kind of thing happened all the time at various levels. As I noted earlier with Cuba, the head White House honcho for Latin America had been spewing secrets to the media and to an uncleared senator. When I worked on Afghanistan, a political appointee at the NSC regularly leaked sensitive policy decisions before the SECRET stamp ink was dry. *The Washington Post* sometimes reported these revelations before the government rank and file was informed. And when working on a White House program that was so secret that we who worked in it had to agree to have our phone conversations monitored and to travel under aliases, leaks from inside the White House made us scramble to cover the potential damage.

Valerie Plame & Me

My book manuscripts must undergo government security review before I can even show them to a book agent or a publisher. Those I published before 2000 were cleared quickly and with little interference from the censors. The Bush-2 administration, however, tightened the process up greatly. It took almost six months to get clearance for my novel, *Tribe*. Upon completion of the manuscript, I phoned State to ask to whom I should send it. In return, they faxed me a letter stating, "Everything you write will be considered classified until cleared by this office."

Four agencies of the federal government needed to have a crack at it. A large intelligence agency had "problems" with it. Worse, so did a major law enforcement agency. The intel agency objected to my description of a well-known training facility. I emailed them links to a Wikipedia article on it as well as commercially produced overhead satellite photography of it; I added transcripts of books which have pages of detailed information on it. The intel agency held its ground and posed additional objections to other elements in my book. Then the law enforcement agency declared they had problems as well. But they refused to reveal what they were, opting instead to stonewall and leave me hanging. Eventually, I managed to negotiate mutually acceptable changes with everybody, but a valuable half-year had passed, leaving several literary agents wanting to see the manuscript cooling their heels.

Despite my cribbing of espionage tradecraft techniques from open sources, I was sure my latest spy thriller, *Havana Queen*, would drive the censors to apoplexy, dyspepsia, tachycardia and a host of other conditions based on Greek-derived medical terms. But I was pleased that the process took a record short six weeks. I confess that I do self-censor somewhat more than I have previously, careful to avoid too much detail about secret stuff. Nonetheless pushing the envelope, as well as the buttons of those in authority, has always been in my nature. A writer, after all, must be honest with himself.

Here's a message from yours truly to Uncle Sam: I'm no danger to our national security. I play by the rules. I'm proud to have served my country loyally. I promise I'll take the real secrets I know to my grave – and you can monitor my mortal remains for preternatural communications with unauthorized celestial beings, if you wish. Just let me write my books and get them published.

More on Censorship: Don't Mess With "The Man" - Two Case Studies

I discussed previously, the arduous security review to which I must submit all of my writings. My novel, *Tribe*, a thriller about Afghanistan was held up for six months as green eye-shaders in the bowels of the federal bureaucracy went through the book line-by-line with an eye toward ensuring I didn't reveal any state secrets. Indeed, four national security agencies had a crack at it. In the end, they made redactions of text and compelled me to change other sections. The good news is that they left the sex scenes untouched. The bad news is I lost a top book agent who ran out of patience waiting for the feds to complete their task (I subsequently acquired another top agent, who also represents Stieg Larsson).

Recently, two cases of government officials bucking this security review process have made the headlines. A veteran CIA case officer who goes by the nom de plume/ cryptonym, "Ishmael Jones," quit his agency three years ago in order to lobby for intelligence reform. The CIA, he wrote, "has become a bureaucratic creature loyal only to itself, with almost unlimited funds and no accountability. Reliance upon it is our major national security weakness." Jones wrote a book about this called, The Human Factor: Inside the CIA's Dysfunctional Intelligence Culture. He had dutifully submitted the manuscript for security review by the CIA. After a year of waiting, Jones proceeded to publish his book without the CIA's permission, his patience with his former agency having run out. He felt the Agency objected to his criticism rather than anything deemed classified. In his blog, Jones writes, "the CIA took the unusual step of disapproving every single word in the manuscript." In my own case, the CIA took the same action, having stamped on the cover sheet: "Deny-CIA Entire Text."

The Agency's approach appears to be one of rejecting an entire manuscript pending necessary redactions and other changes being made. Once I had met their concerns, the CIA censors then gave the green light to the entire manuscript.

The CIA brought a lawsuit against Jones for having published The Human Factor in violation of the review requirement. It will be a David vs. Goliath battle as cash-strapped Jones goes to the courts against an agency with deep pockets.

The other case involves a State Department Foreign Service officer, Peter Van Buren, who, disillusioned with our Iraq policy, wrote a book about his year of service in that country, *We Meant Well: How I Helped Lose the Battle for the Hearts and Minds of the Iraqi People.* Van Buren's book is a "darkly funny tragicomic…voyage of ineptitude and corruption that leaves its writer — and readers — appalled and disillusioned but wiser." Van Buren also did not wait for the official green light and went ahead with publication. The State Department declared its formal objection. Van Buren, who had been reassigned to a career-deadening job in human resources, left the Foreign Service shortly afterward.

When the government gets serious about punishing an employee who bucks the security review process, as well as sending a message to others, it legally garners all the royalties of the offending employee's publication. Frank Snepp, a CIA case officer who, in the 1970's, wrote an exposé about our Vietnam policy, was sued and forfeited his royalties on the book to Uncle Sam.

Jones and Van Buren were idealistic public servants who were sincerely concerned about what they saw as deep shortcomings in the way Washington conducted its foreign affairs. But having messed with "The Man," they ended up paying dearly. Having gone through the review process five times, I can empathize with them regarding the time lost. But, in my own case, I'll stick to the rules and save my energies for promoting and marketing my books.

Censorship: Navy SEAL Faces Charges for Writing Uncleared Book on Bin-Laden Raid

I shipped off to the U.S. State Department my fourth book for security review as required by nondisclosure rules binding on all active duty and retired government personnel who have held top secret security clearances. Taking an average of six months per review, my books will have sat a total of two years with the green eye-shaders in Washington. That's two years of not being published. Two years of royalties not flowing into my bank account.

So, why do I put up with this? Because I have to. The regs state:

Public speeches, writings and teaching materials on matters of "official concern" must be submitted to the appropriate office for review before publication or use. The purpose of such review is to ensure that classified material and other material protected by law are not improperly disclosed.

An employee must not publish any public speaking, writing, or teaching material on a matter of official concern until all classified material has been deleted from the submitted material.

And, as with all USG employees who are granted a security clearance, I signed a nondisclosure agreement requiring me to submit all relevant writings for review prior to publication.

Former CIA ops officer "Ishmael Jones" (a pseudonym) and ex-State Department Foreign Service officer Peter Van

Buren were sanctioned for having violated the rules by publishing uncleared tell-all books. A federal judge ordered Jones to remand all of his royalties to Uncle Sam. The State Department fired Van Buren.

And there is the case of Matt Bissonnette, aka "Mark Owen," a SEAL Team 6 member who participated in the operation to kill Osama bin-Laden. Owen, (also a pseudonym) has written a book about the operation without first getting it cleared by the Defense Department. It is not clear why Bissonnette chose to go this route. He states in the book that he wants "to set the record straight about one of the most important missions in U.S. military history. 'No Easy Day' is the story of 'the guys,' the human toll we pay, and the sacrifices we make to do this dirty job."

Reactions from Special Forces colleagues weren't positive. The unofficial Special Forces website sofrep.com asserted, "Word has it that {Owen} was given the boot from SEAL Team Six's Red Squadron not long after the Bin Laden raid, possibly causing some bad blood. There is also speculation that {Owen} has come on some hard times financially leading him to chase a seven figure payday. Don't tell us the money is for charity because that doesn't give you a free pass." One member added, "members of SEAL Team 6 are extremely angry about this book and feel betrayed."

For its part, Owen's publisher, Dutton, said, "for tactical, technical, and procedural information as well as information that could be considered classified by compilation" by a former "special operations attorney." In response, a Special

Operations Command (SOCOM) spokesman said any such review by a non-USG attorney was "irrelevant."

Media reports almost all missed the point when discussing this case. The talking heads focused on whether or not Bissonnette was spilling sensitive information. They concluded that, if not, then there should be no problem. That's completely wrong. The point is whether Bissonnette violated his legal obligation to clear his writing, as the rest of us must. If so, he can expect to face the same kind of sanctions as have Jones, Van Buren and others before them.

What I find particularly troubling, legal issues aside, is why Bissonnette chose to take the extraordinarily risky step of revealing his own identity, and possibly those of other Team 6 members, by publishing an uncleared book. His real name had been reported early on. A spokeswoman for the publisher said, "Personal security is the sole reason the book is being published under a pseudonym." Who are they kidding? After a few minutes of cyber-sleuthing, I had ascertained "Owen's" address, photo, family relations and other tidbits. If I were an al-Qaeda operative, I'd have a good fix on how to find him. As one of the team members who helped dispatch bin-Laden, Bissonnette is most certainly a wanted man among Islamist terrorist circles. His cavalier approach to his personal "OPSEC" defies common sense.

Bissonnette most assuredly faces a protracted legal battle which will probably result in the royalties of his book being forfeited to the government – notwithstanding that "the majority of the proceeds" from the book will be "donated to charities helping the families of killed SEALs."

So, why does one government official after another snub his nose at Uncle Sam and proceed with publishing uncleared books when the track record shows he will only bring down a world of hurt on himself? Only each individual can answer that.

Censorship: The Travails of a Top Secret Public Servant

Good news: I had finished my latest thriller, *Havana Queen*. Bad news: I had to deal with the federal bureaucracy in getting the book security reviewed and cleared. State Department had sent me the following:

"Text is presumed to be, and handled as classified until cleared. Do not share uncleared text with potential publishers, or anyone else without a security clearance. Even though text contains information concerning other executive branch entities or the White House, you should not contact those agencies directly for clearance.

When clearance is final, you will receive a letter, the cleared version of your manuscript showing required redactions or rewritten text as agreed upon, and our requested disclaimer clause. Any additions or substantive rewrites may require additional review."

Oy veh!

Postscript: the Department cleared my manuscript is record time and the book was published in the summer of 2013

Letter from France

The French have a saying: *On ne change pas un équipe qui gagne.* Literally, it translates to "One does not change a winning team." The English equivalent would be: "If it ain't broke, don't try to fix it." When I left the United States for Europe a couple of years ago, the headlines in the publishing news centered on Border's bookstores going bankrupt and closing all remaining outlets. The nation's biggest chain bookstore, Barnes & Noble, moreover, continues to struggle with its bottom line. The irony, of course, is that big box stores, which drove independent bookstores to near extinction, are themselves now on the ropes, victims of burgeoning online retailing. This kind of often wrenching business transformation is what the economist Joseph Schumpeter termed "creative destruction."

In contrast with the U.S., it seems there is an independent bookstore on virtually every block in Paris. A used book dealer opposite our hotel in Montparnasse was doing a brisk business selling books from stacks piled to the ceiling, a French literary version of the 1970s U.S. TV show about junk dealers, *Sanford & Sons.* A customer would ask the aged Parisian shopowner for, say, an original edition of Breton's *Entretiens.* He'd squint his eyes in concentration, then dive into a stack and pull it out. Other indies in the French capital are spiffy literary boutiques. All appeared successful, thriving small businesses. This goes for the towns as well. The

French love to read. For some reason, they prefer mostly to buy their books from shops. At least so far. But the indies here compete alongside big chains such as Gibert Joseph. Nobody seems to be going under.

This gets to the question of quality of life. In contrast with the U.S., one doesn't see much big box suburban sprawl here and most cities and towns don't look drained of commercial life. The French *centreville* is a vibrant economy of shops and boutiques where the shopper can pick up everything from foies gras to band-aids without schlepping out to the burbs. And the quality is top-notch. Arch-conservative curmudgeons back home rail against "European socialism," how it stymies economic growth and puts Big Brother government into citizens' lives. Well, France has the world's fifth largest and wealthiest economy, the second largest economy in Europe (behind Germany). The French economy took a smaller hit in the 2008-2009 recession and bounced back more quickly. GDP growth has been stronger than expected, at one percent, one of the best performances in Europe. The French are the wealthiest Europeans, accounting for more than a quarter of richest European households. Globally, France ranks as the fourth wealthiest nation, being proportionally the wealthiest as well as one of the least debt-laden. Take that, Mitch McConnell.

Certainly, the French struggle with all manner of problems, political, economic and social. But they, and their European neighbors, offer lessons in quality of life from which Americans can learn. So, as the grand guignol of politics continues to play out like a train wreck in Washington, let's not be so arrogant as to think we Americans have all the answers and that our European friends have nothing to offer us. It's time for the American people to contemplate changing its leadership team. The system indeed is broken and requires fixing. Meanwhile, I'm off to pick up a baguette and cafe au lait, and maybe an original edition of Breton.

Tom Clancy

The difference between fiction and reality? Fiction has to make sense.
~ Tom Clancy.

Thriller writers, but especially military and espionage thriller writers, owe a debt of gratitude to Tom Clancy. Clancy, who died recently, was an originator of the "techno-thriller," fast-moving yarns grounded in current events and chock full of technocratic details that give the reader the sense of being cleared into top secret high-tech weapons and intelligence programs. So accurate are his depictions of the inner workings of national security that the author won many fans from the U.S. military, diplomatic and intelligence establishment, myself included. In the corridors of the Pentagon, CIA and State Department, one would hear water cooler chatter along the lines of, "Who the hell's leaking that intel to Clancy anyway?" President Reagan was one of Clancy's biggest fans.

The Hunt for Red October and the follow-on Jack Ryan films changed the public's image of military and spy-themed action heroes. Prior to Clancy, the spy fiction sphere was dominated, on the one hand, by Ian Fleming and Robert Ludlum, with their super-heroes and far-fetched plots, and, on the other, by John LeCarré, with his more reality-based, yet gloomy, tales of bureaucrats with a license to spy. Clancy brought back the patriot-hero following a long post-Vietnam spell of portraying government operatives in fiction as evildoers. But Clancy's heroes are regular folks who overcome extraordinary challenges with quick minds and high-tech tools. "So, you take an ordinary sort of guy and drop him into a serious situation. It's the same technique Hitchcock used," Clancy said.

Another thing that distinguishes Clancy's thrillers from those by Robert Ludlum and his literary heirs, Vince Flynn, Lee Child and company, is his linking of senior-level policy decisions — at the White House, Pentagon or the CIA — with the highly trained, "ordinary sort of guys" implementing them. Jack Ryan and Jason Bourne are about as different from each other as are a STU-4 secure line from a Glock 19. This accurate describing of how national decisionmaking and implementation function in real life is the central strength of Clancy's fiction. It's thriller writing for the intelligent reader. He said, "I think it's necessary to describe the tools my characters use to lend verisimilitude to my work, which is why I include it. . . . Verisimilitude provides texture that adds to the richness and plausibility of the story." Exactly! This is what I preach at International Thriller Writers' ThrillerFest and in my blog posts. Make it sound real and you've got the reader's attention. To retain his attention, pace the story. "Suspense is achieved by information control. What you know. What the reader knows.

What the characters know. You balance that properly, and you can really get the reader wound up," Clancy said on this point.

As the years went by and his success grew, Clancy seemed to be more businessman than writer, franchising his name out to ghostwriters and videogames. The old Clancy storytelling tautness slackened. There was less technical detail and gripping plotting by those who wrote under the vaunted Clancy name, as reflected in the reviews of the later books. He even turned over his signature Jack Ryan series to ghostwriters. Readers still bought the books, but many took umbrage at the false advertising: "TOM CLANCY" (big letters) "with joe blow" (small letters). It may be unfair to say, but it seemed his heart was no longer in storytelling.

Nevertheless, Clancy's impact on his successors in the thriller genre he inspired will be long term. Like his predecessors, Ian Fleming and John LeCarré, Tom Clancy changed the genre, and those of us who have followed in his literary wake are indebted to him.

The Loneliness of the Long Distance Writer

Annie Wilkes: "God came to me last night and told me your purpose for being here. I am going to help you write a new book."

Paul Sheldon: "You think I can just whip one out?"

Annie Wilkes: "Oh, but I don't think Paul, I know… I'm your number one fan."

~ *from the movie "Misery"*

The deranged Annie Wilkes ends up breaking Paul Sheldon's ankles with a sledge hammer to keep him from escaping and force him to rewrite his latest novel with an ending to her liking. Rewrites are as central to good writing as is completing the initial draft. But it can drive one batty. I rewrote my latest novel, *Havana Queen*, several times, working with a top notch editor and her team. Their red pen slicing and dicing of my manuscript made *Havana Queen* a work I can be really proud of. But, at times, I felt like Annie Wilkes just hobbled me with a four-pound fence post driver.

In my post, *Inspired Insomniac: Voices in the Dark*, I describe the solitary laboring in silence of a writer, how this writer routinely stays up till 3:00 am pecking away at the keyboard. Characters' voices take over my brain as I sit alone in the dark. If you are an extrovert in need of constant social stimulation, forget about becoming a writer. It'll drive you nuts. But, if like me and most serious writers, you're okay spending whole days and weeks shuttered behind closed doors, stooped over a backlit screen, spilling your emotional guts into stories you fantasize will become *New York Times* bestsellers, you can give it a try. Not all will admit it, but your average fiction writer is socially awkward and somewhat delusional, more at home in his or her world of fantasies than in the workaday world most of us must inhabit.

In the hilarious, quirky movie, *Wonder Boys*, the Michael Douglas character, Grady Tripp, is a college professor and has-been novelist whose latest work and personal life are in a rut. Uninspired, the middle aged writer just keeps adding more pointless chapters to a pointless plot. At one point, a

female student gives him some much-needed honest feed-
back: "Even though your book is really beautiful, I mean,
amazingly beautiful, it's... it's at times... it's... very detailed.
You know, with the genealogies of everyone's horses, and
the dental records, and so on. And... I could be wrong, but
it sort of reads in places like you didn't make any choices.
At all. And I was just wondering if it might not be different
if... if when you wrote you weren't always... under the influence." Later in the story, the typewritten paper manuscript,
his only copy, gets blown to the four points of the compass
by a devil's wind in a parking lot. Just as well. It forces him
to make a fresh start as an artist and as a person. Sometimes
it feels the same during a major rewrite. One's labor of love
is blown away in all directions, forcing one to virtually start
over.

Anyway, during my rewrite, I'd put the rest of my life on
hold. The mail piled up. Shaving was sporadic. Communication with friends and fans went dead. Loved ones expressed
guarded concern as to whether I was okay. My punditizing
went fallow. I told them it was all right. Not to worry about
me. I was crashing on my book, soon to be a *New York Times*
bestseller...

SO, SOMEBODY'S GOT TO DO IT

Final Thoughts

The subtitle of this book is, *Why Foreign Policy Should Not Be Left in the Hands of Diplomats, Spies and Political Hacks*. My essays describe a foreign policy and national security establishment seemingly in the hands of a dysfunctional Department of State, bumbling intelligence agencies, a defense establishment with some serious leadership flaws and a White House driven almost solely by political opportunism. Corruption – political, moral and financial – permeate the system, be it sex-addicted generals, insider horse trading over diplomatic posts, brazen selling of ambassadorships, or party animal Secret Service agents. And then there is the rampant incompetence: ambassadors, career and non-career, who put their staff in danger or embarrass the U.S. with their shameful personal comportment; intelligence officers lacking in any common sense; and a Pentagon whose lax security controls enabled an off kilter Army private to release hundreds of thousands of classified documents to a hacker/anarchist who then dumped them on the world. A replay of this sad transgression, of course, came with another grudge-bound hacker, Edward Snowden, whose easy theft and release of countless highly sensitive documents is doing serious damage to this country's national security. In whom can we trust? What happened to the nation that defeated the Axis powers and patiently wore down communism until its inevitable collapse? Are we becoming a banana republic? Who should be running our foreign policy apparatus? As with embalming, radioactive waste site management and accounting, somebody has got to do it. If we can't rely on the diplomats, spies, soldiers and politicians, who then?

Much of my discussion, of course, is tongue-in-cheek, satire that draws on select cases of both faulty leadership and execution meant to drive home a point: that our government is manned by human beings subject to all the thousand natural shocks that flesh is heir to. I also provide examples of outstanding public servants: diplomats who carry out their duties in face of PTSD, injury and death from terrorist acts or serving in war zones; FBI counterintelligence agents who ably protect this country from Russian sleeper agents, al-Qaida and Iranian assassins; and an intelligence community that collects valuable information for our decisionmakers as well as keeps dangerous adversaries like Iran and North Korea off balance. My satire aside, U.S. national security generally is in the hands of serious, qualified and dedicated people. The problem chiefly lies in structure, procedures, recruitment and bloat.

The rapid growth of the national security apparatus post 9/11 has brought with it inefficiencies, redundancies and mismanagement on many levels. The threat challenges are constantly evolving, yet the structures and personnel for dealing with them are not keeping up. That is why the President and Congress need to focus on government reform with an eye toward streamlining and rationalizing structures and responsibilities. I touch on this need to reform in my essays, "What the Foreign Service Can Learn from the U.S. Military," "What's Wrong With America's Generals," and those addressing the diplomatic spoils system. The State Department and Foreign Service, in particular, need to take a fresh look at recruitment, motivation, incentives, staffing and accountability. The military has much to offer in the way it performs these functions.

The way in which the United States sells senior diplomatic positions to political contributors is nothing short of shameful and disgraceful. It is an outmoded practice that needs to end. That is not to say that highly qualified and respected individuals such as Congressman Tom Foley, Senator Howard Baker, and Senator Daniel Patrick Moynihan should not serve this country as noncareer ambassadors to key countries. They possess unique skills, contacts and knowledge that no career diplomat can even approximate. But the corruption of pay-for-play ambassadorships must end. It not only often damages our foreign policy execution; it also makes us look like hypocrites when lecturing other nations on clean and transparent government. Enabling this easy corruption is the American people's woeful ignorance of foreign affairs and those who implement it. I seek to highlight in my essays the woeful lack of knowledge among Americans of their nation's diplomats and what they do. Certainly, a greater public education effort in this area is warranted.

234 | JAMES BRUNO

Finally, I've described my own personal journey from diplomat to full-time writer, a progression which, for me, has been fairly seamless. Having been trained in journalism, writing has always been my passion, one that I was able to continue as a diplomat reporting from my overseas postings and drafting policy analyses and recommendations while serving in Washington. But my transition from government team player to authorial constructive iconoclast is complete and irreversible. I use my fiction as well as my nonfiction to edify, entertain and criticize on matters relating to diplomacy, intelligence and the military. I've turned down a variety of offers to return to the world of suits and ties, commutes and office politics. The pen, after all, is mightier than the paycheck.

James Bruno's Facebook Author Site & Email List Signup:

Go to James Bruno's Facebook page at:
on.fb.me/1qfzXC9

See the author's blog at DIPLO DENIZEN, at
jameslbruno.blogspot.com/

Sign up for James Bruno's Newsletter at
bit.ly/1kCGh5D